Persuasive Business Writing

Persuasive Business Writing

Creating Better Letters, Memos, Reports, and More

Mary Cross

amacom

AMERICAN MANAGEMENT ASSOCIATION

This book is available at a special
discount when ordered in bulk quantities.
For information, contact Special Sales Department,
AMACOM, a division of American Management Association,
135 West 50th Street, New York, NY 10020.

Library of Congress Cataloging-in-Publication Data

Cross, Mary.
    Persuasive business writing.

    Bibliography: p.
    Includes index.
    1. Business writing. I. Title.
HF5718.3.C76 1987   808'.066651   86–47808
ISBN 0–8144–5898–X

Figure 4-1: Egg-o-Mania (by Bob Pliskin)
Reprinted with permission from the February 15, 1985 issue of Advertising Age.
Copyright, Crain Communications Inc., 1985.

Printing number

10 9 8 7 6 5 4 3 2 1

Introduction

The Power of Persuasion

Persuasive business writing is business writing that gets results: replies, decisions, sales, shipments.

The key to such results is persuasion. All business writing needs it, but few people know how to use it or how easily it can be built into letters, memos, and reports.

The word *persuasion* means "to win over," "to convince," "to gain acceptance." In speaking, you know instinctively how to be persuasive. The day you talked your parents out of the family car keys or got your first job or convinced the girl or boy of your dreams to say yes, you were practicing the art of persuasion, and you were good at it.

In writing, persuasion involves the same winning ways. You create a situation that moves readers to choose action, not inertia, and to say yes, not no.

To be persuasive, you must make your readers an offer they can't refuse. That means answering their primary question: What's in it for me? Every technique in this book is designed to help you give motivating answers to that question.

As far back as the fourth century B.C., philosophers such as Aristotle were teaching their disciples how to put the crucial ingredient of persuasion into their speech and writing. Today, at the end of the twentieth century, skill at persuasion is in demand. As a dean at one of the country's leading business schools said recently, "The most important thing people can know is how to motivate others."

In this information age, where messages bounced off satellites move with the speed of light and our knowledge of the world doubles every five years, what we write must carry the power of persuasion just to get noticed.

Being persuasive doesn't take talent, but it does take practice. You've already had plenty of that in your everyday encounters with other people. You've been known to charm the skin off the proverbial snake when you wanted something—a raise, a business deal, a plumber at odd hours, or lunch with an attractive member of the opposite sex.

Yet when it comes to writing, you may draw a blank. For one thing, the audience is unseen, and all the charm of your personal presence goes unnoticed. For another, words get in the way. Writing seems to cramp your style, and you come off sounding stiff and formal, not at all your usual beguiling self.

And now that there are apt to be computers in the office, with the opportunity to send an instant letter electronically, your ability to use language is really on the line, as it were. You could use some verbal strategy that would guarantee results.

Adding the ingredient of persuasion to what you write will increase the chances of getting the response—and the action—you need. Time is money in business, where the ability to make things happen is prized. If you can write the kind of letters, memos, and sales pieces that get results, you can enhance your career as well as your writing.

No one has ever been able to turn writing into an exact science, with a set of formulas that you could pull out whenever you needed them. But there are specific techniques you can learn that will energize any written message with the power of persuasion. They are tricks of the trade that you can use to make your business writing a persuasive, results-oriented tool.

Here are just a few of the things this book will teach you:

- Nothing makes readers act more quickly than does an appeal to their own self-interest.
- Readers tend to remember better what you say when your message is positive.
- You'll get better results if you spell out the action you want rather than let readers draw their own conclusions.
- Being honest about possible drawbacks can win sympathy and acceptance from readers.
- People are never as involved with your written words as you are; you need to overcome an initial disinterest.
- The faster you get to your main point, the better your readers will

understand your entire message and the more readily they'll accept it.

Many of the strategies in this book come from the sales and advertising fields, where persuasion techniques have a proven track record in the marketplace. The same successful techniques used by copywriters to build interest and response will work to energize your letters, memos, and reports with the power of persuasion. Other strategies come from the fields of psychology and behavioral science, where research has increased our understanding of human motivation.

You'll read a lot about readers as customers and about buyer behavior in *Persuasive Business Writing,* since it was written to show you how to make the English language do the work of selling—whether an idea or a product—on paper.

To turn a reader into a customer, you need to know and use the basic techniques in this book. They start with the approach to writing that copywriters call Copythink. Why not turn to Chapter One and get started?

Contents

                 For Further Reading   **171**

                 Notes   **173**

Part One
THE ART
OF PERSUASION

Chapter One

Copythink

Writing, let's face it, is difficult. It requires thinking. That's hard work.

In *Persuasive Business Writing,* however, you'll find both writing and thinking made easier. Here, they are considered as strategies, in the ancient and military sense of planning skillful action. Just as a general positions troops to win a battle, so a writer deploys words to produce a desired effect: win customers, collect money, create goodwill. The management of words in business, like the maneuvering of soldiers in combat, is a matter of strategy.

Strategy, in this book, is a plan of verbal action aimed at producing results. Designing a message to inspire action will make writing more of a challenge and less of an ordeal for you, especially when the right words can bring tangible response from other people and influence them to act.

Copythink

The basic strategy for persuasion is to make your readers an offer they can't, or won't, refuse. This strategy consists not only of how you say it, but what you say. And before you write a word, you must make some crucial decisions about your readers, your message, and your selling point. You have to do a little homework, but no more than any good salesperson or advertising copywriter does in getting ready to sell a product.

Copywriters call this homework "Copythink," a three-step process of analysis that goes on in your head before you write, to help you find the best strategy for selling. Here are the three steps, as advertising uses them:

1. Know your customer.
2. Know your product.
3. Find the Central Selling Point.

In this book, your customer is your reader. Your product is your message. And the Central Selling Point is the persuasive buy-this-and-get-that offer you make to your reader.

These three steps of Copythink are based on the primary transaction that occurs in all writing:

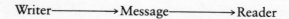

Writer————————→Message————————→Reader

Copythink, however, takes the transaction one step further:

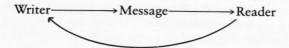

Writer————————→Message————————→Reader

The difference is that in Copythink you want the reader—your customer—to get back to you with a reply, a decision, or a purchase. To get this response, you need to know who your reader is and what your reader wants. You must decide what your message is. And you must find the selling point in your message that will most appeal to your reader's own needs and interests, motivating the response you seek.

The three steps of Copythink are a system for doing your mental homework before you write, whether you spend five minutes on them at your desk or mull them over for several days. They make it easy to find the best selling strategy. And they help you turn readers into real "customers" for the ideas or the message you want to "sell."

Let's take a quick look at each step. Then we'll go into detail about planning persuasive writing based on Copythink.

Know your customer. If there's any secret to persuasion, this is it. Nothing is more important in persuasive business writing than your knowledge of your reader. That person, group, or faraway corporate audience will determine the way you present your message, the kind of language you'll use, and the offer you make for "buying" your proposition or product.

Most of all, knowledge of your reader will help you provide that persuasive echo in your writing of the reader's own attitudes and concerns. This echo gives your writing a familiar sound that tends to lessen the reader's criticism and resistance.

How do you find out about your reader? First, you simply switch your focus from your own concerns as a writer to the concerns of your reader—any reader.

A reader's view of your message will be very different from yours. This stems from a natural self-interest. Remember that the reader isn't sitting around waiting for your letter and probably isn't familiar with your subject. And the reader is very busy.

Writers, immersed in the message from their own point of view, tend to forget the reader's concerns. But there's nothing more important to persuasion than shifting your focus to the reader.

Second, you can ask some objective questions to help you draw a mental picture of your readers even if you've never laid eyes on them. Using the reader analysis checklist in Figure 1–1, you can do a miniprofile on any reader. The who-what-when-where-how-and-why questions will help you focus on the reader's concerns.

For example, it's important to ask what your readers may already know about your subject, to avoid boring them with too much background—or confusing them by not explaining enough. Can the reader act on your message or does he need approval from someone else? How will the reader's job be affected by your message? As you run through the checklist, even if you don't have answers to all the questions, you will, inevitably, find yourself thinking like the reader and gathering important information about him. Getting to know your reader will help you *fit the message to the reader's needs.*

Make it a habit to visualize the person on the other side of your letter, memo, or report. Conjure the reader up mentally, seated at a desk in a business suit, with the telephone ringing, appointments waiting, papers piled up. Your message will have better aim, and get better results.

Know your product. In persuasive business writing, your product is your message. This product is less tangible than a diet cola or a household cleanser. It's an idea for improving sales, a request for payment on a past-due bill, a memo to employees about keeping costs down.

But you still want to sell it. To do that, you have to know your product. Nothing gives you confidence like knowing what you're talking about. And nothing gives you more credibility with your readers than sounding as if you do. Knowledge is powerful in persuasion.

If you were selling a car or a computer, you'd make sure you knew how it worked, what its special features were, and how it stacked up

Figure 1–1.   Reader analysis checklist.

1. WHO?

Job title, department, responsibilities
Length of time with the company
Educational background, specialty
Personal: age, sex, attitudes, hobbies

2. WHAT?

What does the reader already know about the subject?
What else does he/she need to know?
What will the reader do about this message? (decide, delegate, transmit, do the work)
What's in it for the reader? Benefits? Risks?

3. WHEN?

When will he/she read this message?
How much time will the reader spend on it?
When does the reader have to act?

4. WHERE?

Where in the company hierarchy is this reader located? (top management, middle management, branch office, plant worker, secretary, other)
Where does the reader do most of his/her work? (at a desk, at a machine, walking around, or elsewhere)
Where else in the company does the reader have to go for approval to act?

5. HOW?

How interested is the reader in the arrival of this message?
How will the reader feel about it? (good news or bad news)
How will the reader's job be affected by this message?

6. WHY?

Why am I writing?
Why should the reader respond?

against the competition. You'd anticipate the customer's questions and have some answers ready. You'd get to be an expert.

In persuasive business writing, you need to be an expert, too. It's even more important, since you and your customer—the reader—can't see each other. You won't get the instant feedback that you can count on in a face-to-face encounter.

Just as you've researched your reader, you must learn everything you can about your product. Be sure that you have all the information you need before you write. Even if you're just writing a routine memo to your staff, it won't hurt to collect your thoughts and refresh your memory about how you've handled things in the past.

Next, ask yourself, What is my message here? You'd be surprised at how many writers never ask themselves that question (or maybe you wouldn't be, having had to wade through too much muddled prose already).

Then, make a list of all the other related points that you need to add. Finally, using one of the three formats for persuasion in Chapter Three, organize what you have to say.

Find the Central Selling Point. There's one thing on the reader's mind as she reads: What's in this for me? And the one thing that will move her to respond, accept, or decide to buy is your answer: Buy this and get that. That is selling's basic proposition, the Central Selling Point. It links what you want to what the customer wants.

To find the Central Selling Point, pick the most important feature of your idea, plan, request, or product. Then, focusing on the reader, think about ways this feature can benefit that reader. For example, if you are writing a letter of application for a job, pick your strongest qualification and turn it into a benefit for the prospective employer: *"My five years as a sales manager mean that you would be hiring an experienced executive who could learn your markets quickly."*

If you're writing a letter to collect money that a customer owes you, remind the customer that payment will restore lost credit privileges or maintain a good credit rating.

The Central Selling Point helps make your message real to the reader. It's like a free sample. Because the Central Selling Point is tailored to the reader, it helps the reader "own" your ideas. It brings reader and message together for maximum motivation and response.

Preparation is the whole story in selling. By following these three steps, you'll do the homework—the thinking—that sets up your strategy for persuasive business writing.

Now, let's take a closer look at each of the three steps of Copythink.

Know Your Customer

Consumer behavior is what makes stock markets fall, retail sales soar, and economic conditions unpredictable. It's what sweeps one candidate into office on a landslide and turns another down in the primary. And it is the hidden ingredient in the success or failure of every new product that hits the market. Analyzing this key ingredient of political, social, and economic situations has become big business. Advertising agencies devote large sums of money and time to market research and demographic studies. The persuasiveness of their ads depends on their knowledge of the customer.

This knowledge is just as important to the success of business writing. But you don't need a Gallup poll or a team of researchers to figure out your reader. Adjusting your focus to think about the reader is half the battle. You have to tune in to the reader's all-absorbing mind-set if you want to sell.

The checklist in Figure 1–1 will help you analyze any business reader. You may not be able to find answers to all the questions all the time, but just asking them will give you a better idea of the person you're writing to.

Analyze the Business Reader

Business readers, like all other kinds of readers, have tunnel vision. They tend to select out of your message the part that's most relevant to their own concerns. Your message gets its competitive edge among these readers by acknowledging one truth at the beginning: *Business readers are most interested in their own jobs, status, and power base.*

Thus, just knowing the reader's job title can be an important clue; the president of a company has different concerns than the assembly line worker. People in the finance department have an innate interest in the bottom line. Engineers are going to want to know about specifications. And the sales manager cares most about ways to reach the market.

By using a few objective questions, the who-what-when-where-how-and-why kind that journalists routinely use to gather the news, you can zero in on your reader's special interests. This won't, usually, take any legwork; you can do most of your "research" in your head, right at your desk.

Answers to the "who" questions will give you a miniprofile of your reader's major concerns. Don't worry if you can't get the personal information; a name, an address, and a job title may be all you need to begin picturing the reader.

The "what" questions help you figure out how much explaining you have to do and how to tailor the message to the reader's sphere of influence. And, as we know, the "what's-in-it-for-me?" question is primary in persuasion.

"When" questions help you picture the reader actually reading and suggest how urgent your message must be to motivate the reader to act.

"Where" questions focus on the reader's environment and help you consider the chain of command and other readers who may see your message. Communication in business, for example, typically moves three ways: up, to the people you are accountable to; down, to those you supervise; and sideways, to your peers at the same managerial level. At each of these levels, readers have different concerns that your message must acknowledge.

For example, readers in the top echelon of management usually have a larger stake in the organization and more power to make things happen. They are more concerned with the company's image and success, especially as it affects their own power base, and they are used to delegating authority.

Employees you supervise care about the company, too, and do much of its work. But their interest may be narrowed to their own specific job, and much of their job satisfaction may come from working conditions, their relationship with you, and a paycheck.

Writing to your peers in the company structure is made easier, usually, by the fact that you've had daily contact, perhaps even years of it. It will be easier to do a reader analysis, since your knowledge of your own job, its pressures, and your influence will be a guide.

Finally, the "how" and "why" questions suggest strategy. Their answers may indicate that you'll need to make an extra effort to get the reader's attention, for example, and show you how to organize the message for maximum impact.

Of course, you may already know many of the people you write to very well; and you won't have to run through this checklist every time, for example, that you write your daily memo to your staff. But a rundown on these six areas is guaranteed to make you more aware of the person on the receiving end of your message.

For many of the questions on the checklist, you will have to make assumptions. For instance, you can probably assume that another executive at your level is going to be working at a desk in an office where time is set aside for reading and answering mail. A plant supervisor, on the other hand, might do a lot of moving around and less paperwork.

You may not have access to information about your readers' educational levels or the amount of time they've been with the company.

Age, attitudes, and other personal information are even harder to come by. But, for example, you might assume that the head chemical engineer is older than some of his staff, that he has been out of school longer and may not rely on a textbook approach so much anymore, and that he has been with the company long enough to be in a high-level position.

Use reader analysis in persuasive business writing. Assume that you are a vice president at company headquarters, writing a letter to another vice president at your West Coast office. The West Coast vice president is in charge of marketing in that area, and your letter will ask her to test market a new product the company plans to manufacture. By running through the checklist for analyzing readers, you come up with the following profile:

WHO: The vice president of marketing is a woman named Amy Smith. You have never met her, but you have talked to her on the telephone and received letters from her. From these brief encounters, you know her to be pleasant in most matters but very protective of her territory and stubborn in negotiation. She has been with the company barely three years, you recall, coming in with an M.B.A. and working her way up quickly.

WHAT: She oversees test marketing in the West Coast area, and has done it for the company before. She already knows about the new product and has helped research markets for it. This will be an opportunity for her to show what her marketing staff can do, an important benefit you should emphasize.

WHEN: Because you are writing from the company's headquarters, Ms. Smith will undoubtedly pay close attention to your letter. However, you are asking her to add this marketing project to an already tight schedule of new-product introductions, and she will be pressed for time.

WHERE: As a vice president, she has a good view of the company's overall objectives and structure. She does not need approval from anyone else to implement your request.

HOW: She will be very much interested in your request because it directly affects her job, but will find it

WHY: inconvenient and difficult to fit into her schedule; she may even resent having to run so many marketing projects at once this spring. But doing this one well will be very important evidence of her value to the company. If it works, she will get a lot of the credit.

WHY: You are writing not only to make the request, but to convince her that the project has to be undertaken immediately. She will do it, but may try to reschedule it or put it off. You don't want that to happen.

Now, take your answers to these questions and start visualizing your reader. Actually try to picture her. Imagine her reading your letter at her desk.

You recognize that your reader is not, initially, going to be overjoyed with your message. If you play up its potential benefits, she will be more receptive and willing to cooperate. Because she is fairly new to the company, she may be slightly unsure about her power base and status, and perhaps defensive about taking on extra work. But since you are on an equal basis as vice presidents, you can sympathize, mentioning the extra work this means for everyone.

The reader profile you've just drawn will give your letter considerably more selling power than if you simply wrote and told her what you wanted done.

Instead, you can echo her concerns about time, pressure, and doing a good job; you can get her involved personally by focusing on what success will mean to her track record and how important this project is to the company's future. Your knowledge of this reader will earn you her attention, and quite possibly her prompt acceptance, because you have been able to connect with her own attitudes so well.

Write to more than one reader. When you are writing to persuade, you must also consider other readers who may see your message. The letter you write to the chairman of the board may be sent on to a subordinate and in turn to a staff team for eventual action. Especially with computers and electronic mail systems, your writing may have a much wider audience than you initially project. Don't take for granted that all your readers will have the same background and the same interest in your subject; any reader profile you do should allow for potential differences.

There's a trick to this, one that advertising copywriters use when they write ads to reach many different customers. It's called a One-Customer Profile.

Generate a One-Customer Profile. When you write to more than one person, you can simplify your reader analysis with a composite profile. List all the possible readers for your message. Then run through the reader analysis checklist (Figure 1–1), looking for similar or overlapping concerns. Pick out the major interests and do a One-Customer Profile, creating a picture of an "ideal" reader.

Think about who has to "buy" your idea, who would buy it if they knew about it, and who wouldn't care one way or another. In advertising, for example, ads are aimed at a target audience of the most likely prospects, a composite customer portrayed as a young professional or a working mother, perhaps. Not everyone who reads the ad or buys the product will fall into one of these categories, but a composite has a wider appeal.

Say, for example, that you have an idea for reorganizing the employee benefit plan that you would like to present. Your proposal will go first to your boss, but you know that it will be passed on to various other readers who must consider it. You compose a One-Customer Profile of your "ideal" reader, knowing that everyone in the company will be affected by a change in benefits, even though such a change must first be approved by top management.

Some executives who read your proposal will care about how the change will affect the balance sheet and how it compares with what other companies offer employees. Others will be more personally involved, wondering how it will affect their own lives and paychecks. You decide that your composite reader will be someone whose main concern is financial, and you focus on how your plan will improve both company and personal finances. Although your proposal will reach many different readers, it will be tuned to sound a responsive chord in each of them.

The One-Customer Profile helps you imagine readers more easily as you write, without leaving anyone out. It also helps you address audiences outside the business community.

Write to a general audience. Here, you won't have the rather homogeneous corporate culture to draw on. Instead, you must rely on your knowledge of human nature. For, wherever they work, live, and play, your readers have in common their overwhelming interest in a very human concern: themselves. And the mere act of turning your attention to them will give your writing built-in human interest.

Objective information from the reader analysis checklist can give you helpful leads. Occupational and educational background are valuable clues to a general-audience profile. Keep in mind that the increase in the number of people going to college means that the mass audience is better educated and more sophisticated than it used to be. Increased affluence has broadened people's horizons with more travel and leisure-time activities.

Knowledge of where your readers live and work will help you adjust your message to their concerns. For example, people who live in rural areas miles from the nearest neighbor will have different needs than will those in high-rise city apartments who don't even know their neighbors.

Two of the most important gauges of attitude are age and gender. For example, the age group that advertisers are most interested in these days is 34 to 54 years old, people in their prime earning and spending years. Overlapping into this group is the now-aging Baby Boom generation, born in the surge of population growth after World War II and now making up one-third of the population. As this generation gets older, the total number of people moving into senior citizenship, with a different set of needs and attitudes, will be the largest in history.

The change in female styles of life, marked by the entry of women into the work force in large numbers, requires new selling strategies for both men and women. Many people are delaying marriage and babies until careers are established; meanwhile, they may have more money to spend and different values than those who are already married and raising families.

One advertising research director has observed, in fact, that the last two decades of social upheaval have left Americans with a "Rubik's Cube of values," citing these trends in the general audience:[1]

More prudent consumerism
More interest in personal and physical development
Materialism and feelings of entitlement
Less moral restraint
Environmentalism
Nostalgia for the past

The business of analyzing the consumer and targeting a specific audience becomes more difficult as markets become fragmented and complex. But even though you aren't going to do a major demographic study of readers every time you write, you can use the One-Customer Profile to gauge their major concerns. Flesh out your composite customer from the reader analysis checklist. Imagine your reader's needs, wishes, aspirations. Picture your reader at home reading your letter or at the office browsing through your brochure.

By imagining the reader, you can design a message to appeal to the concerns the reader most identifies with and start to make the reader care about what you say.

David Ogilvy underscores this point with the story of two advertising executives who were arguing over the right length for ad copy. The advertising manager bet his boss, Max Hart, that he could write a whole newspaper page of copy that would make Hart want to read every word. "I'll only tell you the headline," he said: "THIS PAGE IS ALL ABOUT MAX HART."[2]

Know Your Product

In persuasive business writing, words are what you are really selling. And, with your reader profile in hand, you must now turn your attention to deciding what to say.

The best way to get your mental cogs in gear for writing is to collect all the information you need first. Review and get to know it thoroughly. Writers who feel "blocked" often discover that it's because they didn't know enough about their subject to start with. Before you answer a letter, for example, take time to check your files to refresh your memory about any previous correspondence with the writer. A quick scan and a little reflection will help you focus your response.

Some things you write will require real research—a proposal to open a new branch office in another state, for example. Gather all the information, bone up on background, and rehearse the facts and figures that will make your proposal a knowledgeable one. Don't take anything for granted. But don't risk boring the reader with obvious information. Readers aren't mind readers, either. Your reader profile will give you guidelines on how much or how little you have to explain.

Be ready with answers to possible objections or questions. You can disarm the reader at the start, for example, by admitting to some small weakness in your plan or idea; this builds the perception that you are being objective.

When you have done your homework and know your subject, your reader can sense it and will be more willing to trust and believe in what you say.

Stick to One Big Idea

Once you have collected and reviewed your data, you must ask yourself one all-important question: What is my message here? You're looking for the One Big Idea that will stand out, the one thing you want your reader to know and to remember.

As the authors of the best-selling management study *In Search of Excellence* remind us, "Human beings are not good at processing large streams of data and information."[3] Most people, they say, can hold only six or seven pieces of data in mind at once without forgetting something. Thus, it's important to present your message as simply as possible. Readers tend to reduce it to manageable size themselves anyway. So, you might as well make your message easy for them to remember by reducing it yourself, first.

Take your answers to the "why" questions on the reader analysis checklist—"Why am I writing?" and "Why should the reader respond?"—as a guide.

For example, let's say you are writing to apply for a job. That's one answer to the first question. You are also writing to convince the prospective employer that you are the best candidate for the job. That's another answer. And every job application is a request for an interview. That is a third answer.

Now, write these answers as one sentence: *I'm writing to convince the employer that I am the best candidate for this job and should be interviewed for it.* Next, boil it down some more, to get to the One Big Idea: *I'm writing to convince the employer to interview me.*

Now, write some answers to the second "why" question, "Why should the reader respond?" Make a list of the best qualifications on your résumé:

- M.B.A. in accounting
- Six years of experience in the accounting department of a major corporation
- Speaking knowledge of Spanish and work with several Latin American firms

Match these qualifications with those the employer has listed in his advertisement:

- M.B.A.
- Experienced accountant
- Ready for executive position in international department

Why should the reader respond? Because your message echoes his needs. Here's the One Big Idea for your letter: *I am writing to ask for an interview because I have the degree and the experience in accounting you're looking for.*

With a few adjustments, this idea can become your first paragraph: "*My M.B.A. in accounting and my international experience with XYZ*

Corporation may be just what you're looking for in your new vice presi-
dent. I am writing to ask if we might discuss the position in an interview,
at your convenience."

Make a Scratch Outline

The One Big Idea method is a good way to get yourself moving
when you can't think of anything to say and need to generate ideas.
Sometimes, however, you may have too many ideas competing for attention and need to sort them out. An informal scratch outline will help you
set priorities.

Write down all your thoughts, in any order. You can sort them out
better if they are all down on paper in front of you because the human
brain works best visually. When you can see your thoughts, you can organize them.

Next, number them in the order of their importance to you.

Now, go back and number them again, this time in the order of their
probable importance to your reader (keep your reader profile handy).
This should be the organization you use for your message.

For example, here is the off-the-cuff list of things a retail merchan-
dise manager wants to put in a memo:

~~New showroom hours~~
  2 Agenda for buyers' meeting Thursday
  1 Reminder about buyers' meeting
  3 Deadline for orders after meeting
  ~~Problem with employee lateness at lunchtime~~

Numbered according to his own concerns, the list looks like this:

  2 Reminder about buyers' meeting
  1 Agenda for buyers' meeting Thursday
  3 Deadline for orders after meeting

He's already decided to omit two items and save them for another memo,
realizing that they have nothing to do with the One Big Idea of this one.

Next, as he considers the readers' concerns, the priorities change:

  2 Agenda for buyers' meeting
  ~~Reminder about buyers' meeting~~
  1 Deadline for orders after meeting

Recognizing that his readers are most concerned about their own jobs and schedules, the writer will begin with the information most relevant to his readers, the order deadline. That way, he can motivate their attendance at the meeting as well.

> Don't forget that purchase orders for September will be due on the 24th of this month. Be sure to attend the buyers' meeting this week in my office, on Thursday at 2 P.M., so that you can preview the merchandise.
>
> Bring your weekly report to this meeting, too, so that we can run through it before the buyers present. See you Thursday.

More formal outlines are not, except for reports, really necessary in persuasive business writing. The scratch outline and your reader profile will help you find the best way to organize most messages. And, as Chapter Three will illustrate, there are also special formats that can organize any message instantly for maximum persuasive impact.

Find the Central Selling Point

You want to "sell." Your reader will "buy"—change attitudes, act, pay—when she perceives what you are selling as rewarding to her. To bring the "buy" and the "sell" together, pick the main feature of your idea, plan, or product, and turn it into a benefit for the reader. This Feature = Benefit equation is your Central Selling Point.

Translate Feature into Benefit

What's special about what you have to say? What will make it stand out for the business reader already on information overload? What is there about your idea that holds a reward for the reader? As you gather information and organize your message, constantly look for ways to connect it to your reader. What does it stand to offer? Does it satisfy a need or desire? Does it solve a problem?

Your proposal to improve the communications flow in your office could feature the new printed memo forms that can be used for all customer replies. *Benefit:* The staff can answer mail faster and easier.

Your idea for improving sales in a sluggish territory will involve more travel for salespeople, but more exposure to new clients. *Benefit:* Salespeople will have the opportunity to earn bigger commissions.

Even a routine request can have a special feature: it can be brief. *Benefit:* It saves time for the reader.

The idea is to get the reader into the act. The benefit you offer makes your message real and rewarding to her. When she "owns" it this way, she will feel more at home with it. Familiarity takes some of the risk out of buying.

Dramatize: Sell Use

Your Central Selling Point, matching feature to benefit, is like a free sample of what you are offering. And customers love free samples. To talk benefits in your writing, dramatize the Central Selling Point. Show the reader how it will work in her life. Sell use.

Picture your staff using the new memo forms: "*You'll be able to answer your customers' requests in half the time with these new forms.*" Show them how it will work if they "buy" your idea: "*Your new sales route will give you contact with dozens of new clients and bring in more commissions.*"

Advertising copy is designed to sell use. For example, David Ogilvy wrote the most famous of all automobile ads this way, by talking about how it would feel to ride in the car he was selling: "*At 60 miles an hour the loudest noise in this new Rolls-Royce comes from the electric clock.*"[4] A sample-in-print like this is extremely persuasive, recreating your offer as part of the reader's own experience. It gives readers practice in agreeing to your proposition and makes it believable. For example: "*If we had a branch office in Flagstaff, we could tap into a large market of new investors in this rapidly growing Sunbelt state.*" Or: "*My experience in public relations would mean you'd never have to hire outside help again to run your store promotions.*" Or: "*We'd like to keep you as a paying customer, enjoying the full privileges of a charge account at Blossomdale's.*"

Selling use and dramatizing the Central Selling Point depend on your skill at imagining your reader. The more you know about him, the easier it will be to find a benefit to appeal to his needs or solve his problem.

Build the message on benefits. Sell use.

Use the Central Selling Point

Suppose you have opened your own small business, a copy service, in your hometown. You want to write a letter to potential customers telling them about it.

You have decided that your main customers will be other small firms in town and walk-in customers. You would also like to let two large corporations and the bank know that you're open for business. Doing a One-Customer Profile, you decide that all four groups of potential customers have one thing in common: they need fast, handy copy service.

Because your shop is located right on Main Street in the middle of the business district, it is convenient for all these customers. And, because you plan to be open from 8 A.M. to 8 P.M., you can offer your service before and after regular work hours.

Write out some phrases to connect product feature with reader benefit. Sell use:

Fast and handy: Copy Quick
Your new neighborhood copy center
Copies when you need them, right next door

You decide that the last phrase expresses your best Central Selling Point. This gives you a solid selling strategy, bringing customer and product— reader and message—together for maximum motivation.

The Strategy for Persuasion

The three steps of Copythink are a system for thinking about your reader, your message, and your offer before you write. They will help you design the best strategy for persuasion, tailored for each reader and each message.

Chapter Two
Ten Rules
for Persuasion

As you've learned, the three steps of Copythink make up the basic approach you should follow whenever you tackle a piece of business writing. In this chapter, you'll learn ten important rules that can make all the writing you do more persuasive and effective.

The WHAT of Persuasion

The first five rules of persuasion all deal with *what* to say in persuasion. Here's an overview of them.

1. Echo the reader. The echo rule of persuasion goes back more than 2,000 years to the Greek philosopher Aristotle, who was one of the first to write about the art of persuasion. To win people over, Aristotle advised, make your case in terms of *their* thoughts, beliefs, and attitudes— not your own.

He was on to something. People are more likely to accept messages that echo what they already believe. What you say sounds familiar and acceptable right away.

The key to persuasion is what's already in the reader's head, not in whatever it is you're "selling." The "echo" of themselves people hear in your writing is attention-getting, and very convincing. In a nutshell, that's what "echoing" the reader is all about.

2. Fit the message to the reader's needs. This means finding a "fit" between what you want and what your reader wants. By analyzing your

The Ten Rules of Persuasion

What

1. Echo the reader.
2. Fit the message to the reader's needs.
3. Build the message on benefits.
4. Sell use.
5. Spell out action.

How

1. Stick to the one big idea.
2. Talk the reader's language.
3. Play up the positive.
4. Paint the picture with colorful nouns and active verbs.
5. Use short words, sentences, and paragraphs.

readers, you can present your ideas in powerfully persuasive terms, filling a need for the reader.

3. Build the message on benefits. People are motivated by incentives. That's why you offer a reward or benefit for response to your message.

4. Sell use. Show readers how your idea will actually work in their lives. This helps them "own" it, an important step in motivation.

5. Spell out action. Always suggest to readers the action you want them to take. This greatly increases the chances of their taking that action. If you don't spell out the action, readers tend to do nothing or to lose interest.

The HOW of Persuasion

Rules 6 to 10 tell you how to put persuasion into words.

6. Stick to one big idea. Pick your most important point and organize the entire message around it. Your message will have greater impact and reader retention if you don't fragment your reader's attention with too many points.

7. Talk the reader's language. In general, use an informal, natural style to give the effect of a conversation with your reader. The reader will accept and respond faster because the language is familiar. Don't use jargon or special terminology unless you're sure your reader will understand it.

8. *Play up the positive.* Readers accept and remember the positive, ignore or forget the negative. To get your reader to *say* yes, *talk* yes.

9. *Paint the picture with colorful nouns and active verbs.* The effectiveness of persuasion depends on clear, specific images that help the reader visualize your ideas. Abstract words and passive verbs can be ambiguous and boring. Use concrete nouns and active verbs to help the reader experience your thoughts as vividly as you do.

10. *Use short words, short sentences, and short paragraphs.* Always make what you have to say look easy to read. Short, familiar words, sentences in a range of 17 to 22 words, and paragraphs abbreviated for emphasis promise busy readers what they want—fast, easy reading.

Now, let's explore these ten rules in more detail.

Echo the Reader

Ever notice how sometimes it's hard to get an advertising jingle out of your head? Maybe that's because advertising jingles, with their rehearsal of our familiar beliefs and attitudes—"You deserve a break today"—are a perfect example of how the first step in persuasion works.

Advertising jingles and slogans are built on the basic truth that a reassuring echo of the customer's own viewpoint is a surefire way to involve the customer with a message. For example, when MCI was looking for a new advertising slogan, it found that customers weren't blaming the telephone companies for their high bills. They blamed themselves for talking too long. MCI's new slogan echoed this customer concern: "You're not talking too much, just spending too much."

Products as different as IRAs, Cabbage Patch dolls, Hershey bars, and adjustable rate mortgages are sold on the same direct hookup to something customers are already thinking about. The starting place for persuasion is your appeal to the reader's familiar mind-sets. As the perfume, car, and fast-food ads demonstrate, this includes appealing to the reader's self-image, which may be something of an ideal or fantasy.

Advertising uses celebrities to echo this idealized image, implying, perhaps, that if you buy a car from Lee Iacocca or perfume from Catherine Deneuve, you share in some of their star quality. Remember that customers—and readers—accept a message more readily when it echoes who they are, who they think they are, or who they would like to be.

The trick, of course, is to figure out who your reader—your customer—is for everything you write. You have to get a good picture of the people on the other side of your message, even though you can't see them. In advertising, this is known as demographics, finding the target audience. Once you have sighted that target, you can take aim and design a message custom made for results.

Notice how television commercials are aimed at a specific customer. Take the beer ads, for instance. Some are designed to appeal to an audience of the young and affluent, depicting upscale environments and lifestyles. Others—"For all you do, this Bud's for you"—echo a specifically male, often blue-collar audience. Though the ads are different, both talk a particular customer's language, appeal to an image the customer identifies with—and sell lots of beer.

These commercials are the result of extensive market research to find out who the target audience is for a product. On a much smaller scale, you can do the same thing every time you write. *The key is to imagine the reader's point of view, not just your own.*

Everything you need to know about persuading your reader is already in that reader's head. Your written message has to give off signals that it is immediately relevant to the reader's self-interest. In this sense, the customer is always right.

With the knowledge of human behavior that you've already acquired in everyday life, you can make a pretty good thumbnail sketch of the person who is your reader. How, for example, do you think he will react to what you say? What kind of stake does he have in the subject you discuss? Even if you know only your reader's job title, you can understand some important things about him.

The echo rule is really an outgrowth of the first step in Copythink: Know your customer. The technique you learned in Chapter One for analyzing your reader will help you put this rule into action. As Dale Carnegie said fifty years ago, most people spend 95 percent of their time thinking about themselves. "The big secret of dealing with people," he said, "is to devote some of your time to thinking about them."[1] Echo your reader.

Fit the Message to the Reader's Needs

Once you have an idea of who your reader is, you must look for ways to connect your message with something the reader already needs or wants. This energizes the message with a powerful motivation.

People have needs which they naturally seek to satisfy. That's where your message has to operate, making readers aware of their needs and offering to fulfill them. Countless businesses have foundered because they failed to recognize this basic principle. Most makers of "home computers" in the early 1980s, for example, ended up with large unsold stocks because they couldn't show customers why they needed one. "User friendly" as the computer may be, the customer couldn't figure out what to use it for, and sales reflected this.

Customers and readers find it hard to care about something they don't need. Yet they may not recognize a need for something until you've made them aware of it. People buy not only actual items, but what they represent. For example, your neighbor down the street who buys a new car every year doesn't need it for transportation as much as he thinks he needs the status of having the latest model. He could get around just as well in a jalopy, but the need here isn't four wheels—it's the one-upmanship of being first on the block with the latest.

In terms of buyer behavior, this means that people will seek satisfaction for an imagined need as well as for the real thing. They're just as interested in the sizzle as in the steak, sometimes more so if it connects to an idealized self-image.

Your job in persuasion is to help readers become aware of their needs, real or imagined. As you analyze a business audience, for example, you should be alert to the potential for satisfying needs related to such issues as status, self-esteem, and belonging. These are especially powerful appeals to business readers.

Your offer to satisfy a need not only has a strong motivational appeal for readers, but carries an additional emotional appeal. As every communication expert from Aristotle on down has noted, emotional appeals are effective in persuasion because they get people aroused enough to care about what you say. Showing readers that you understand their needs is a good and creditable way to involve them emotionally in your message.

Build the Message on Benefits

To persuade, you must offer an incentive, a reward for action. We're all familiar with Pavlov's dog. You remember the scientist named Pavlov who trained his dog to respond to the sound of a bell by offering it a reward—tasty tidbits. Eventually, the promise of the reward was so motivating that the mere sound of the bell could make the dog's mouth water. Rewards, Pavlov surmised, are the key to motivation.

It gets a little more complicated with human beings. But people also get more involved when there is a reward for doing so. In persuasive business writing, you need to spell out the reward or satisfaction. Remember, the reader's first question is, What's in it for me? Your message must answer that question by describing the benefits of accepting and acting on what you say.

Certain benefits are especially appealing to business readers. They are attracted by a product, a service, or an action that promises they will:

Save time	Receive a discount for
Save money	prompt payment
Make money	Achieve higher status
Cut down on work	Avoid trouble
Improve their overall	Protect their jobs
productivity	Be like the others
Solve a problem	Stand out from the others

In addition, the following attention-getting words and phrases will promote reader interest:

Proven track record	Unique
Fast delivery	New
Revolutionary	Free

Show your reader that the action you suggest can bring rewards. In a letter to a prospective employer, for example, you'll be more persuasive if you point out how the company will benefit by hiring you, rather than if you merely list your own stellar qualifications. And in a memo to employees about the newly installed computer system they'll have to learn, point out the potential of computers for making their jobs easier.

Sell Use

The closer your message gets to the reader's own real-life experience, the more readily the reader will accept it. When you build the message on benefits, make them real to the reader.

Sell use. Show the reader how your idea or product will actually work in his life. Talk about what it will be like to own or use what you're selling.

Dramatize the benefits with a sample-in-print of how much better, easier, more exciting the reader's life will be. By describing your idea in actual use, you help your reader "own" it, and that's a big step toward persuasion. The fragrance companies hit pay dirt when they started to use scent strips for perfume and after-shave lotion in their magazine ads. People could try out the product before they bought it.

Your sample-in-print will work the same way. Talk about how your proposal to put your sales force on commission will give salespeople more independence on the job. Plug the idea for opening a branch office in the suburbs by describing the untapped market of eager customers out there. Remind the reader of the value of a good credit rating when you ask for payment.

Advertisements for cars describe how it feels to be behind the wheel. Supermarkets offer "one-stop shopping." Diet food ads remind you how thin you'll be.

Customers love free samples. Give your readers a sample-in-print. Sell use.

Spell Out Action

The payoff in persuasion is customer action—a decision, a purchase, an agreement. Your reader will "buy" your idea in proportion to your echo of familiar attitudes, your understanding of the reader's needs, and your offer of a motivating benefit.

But the final stage in the persuasion process is showing the customer or reader what to do—and how to do it. Behavioral scientists say that the moment of decision is made easier for people when you show them what the desired action is rather than leave it up to them.

Spell out what you'd like the reader to do in response to your message. You'll have a better chance of getting the action you want. Otherwise, behavioral studies show, your reader may misunderstand or actually lose interest in the entire message.

Make the Action Easy and Make It Urgent

No one likes to make decisions: there is always a risk involved. The trick is to make your reader's decision seem simple and less risky.

You should round off the persuasion process in your letters or memos by suggesting an easy way for the reader to move in your direction. Give him a telephone number to call, enclose an envelope for the check, arrange a date to meet, invite him to lunch; these easy ways to respond will give the reader some momentum. Your suggestion can be as simple as "I look forward to hearing from you," or as motivation-rich as a discount for prompt payment.

Most direct-mail pieces are designed to make response simple. They include an already-addressed postcard, for example, to drop in the return mail. Or they ask you to put a little gummed sticker on the piece or to check a box, on the theory that once you're moving, you'll go all the way to a decision.

Make action urgent, too. Set a deadline for response; tell when you must hear from the reader or when the sale or discount ends. Even the well-worn words "Act now" can instill the feeling of urgency that will move a reader to respond.

The end of a message is the most emphatic place to mobilize action. Your last paragraph is the last thing the reader sees, and the one she's most likely to remember. Don't waste it with personal asides or thanks to the reader for something she hasn't done yet. Spell out action.

Put Persuasion into Words

In all of this, it's clear—with apologies to Marshall McLuhan—that the message is the medium of your persuasive strategies. The way you put together a verbal sales package—what you say and how you say it—determines your success.

Actually, the most effective persuasion takes place face-to-face because you can bring so many other factors into play, including facial expressions and instant feedback. Yet, in both speaking and writing, it is the special effects of language that clinch the deal and determine how persuasive you are.

Your message has to contain verbal "cues" that prompt a reader to get involved—or not—with what you say. These cues are words that get attention, arouse interest, and motivate. They have to be easily understood, believable, and tuned to the reader's own viewpoint.

It's a tall order. In writing, words have to work twice as hard to connect with the unseen reader, who wants information in the easiest possible way. You have to attract readers who threaten at any moment to be distracted or bored or to say, "So what?"

To some extent, all writing is selling. You are persuading your reader to read. You are selling your words.

Rules 6 to 10 spell out the kind of salesmanship-in-print you'll need to be persuasive.

Stick to One Big Idea

There's seldom more than one selling point in a successful ad. "A customer tends to remember just one major claim," Rossner Reeves, author of *Reality in Advertising,* advised.[2] Research by psychologists and communications experts backs him up; our capacity to retain information is limited to about six or seven pieces of data at a time.[3]

For maximum persuasion, you should organize your message around just one main point. Keep it simple. A simple message, for one thing, doesn't get distorted. And readers like to take it easy. They'd like you to do all the work of boiling down the concept and serving it up in an easily digested form.

Because if you don't, they will. As in gossip, people tend to be reductive, going for the jugular in the simplest version of your complex love life and getting rid of complexity in one swift, sensational blow to the reputation. The same thing can happen to your beautifully subtle argument.

Keep it simple. That's more difficult to do sometimes than to write for pages. But it pays off. Your One Big Idea will help readers get your message in the way you intend.

Talk the Reader's Language

We all use the same English language, yet words can mean quite different things to each of us. Our own real-life experience can affect our perception of meaning.

Even though we can all agree, for example, on the basic meaning of the word *money,* it will conjure up a different image in the minds of the rich than in those of the poor. If Eskimos have twenty-six words for snow and none for bikini, that's because, where they live, snow is important and bathing attire isn't usually required. Real estate ads use the word *homes* for the houses they sell because it translates into a more motivating image for most people.

To allow for these differences in perception, your message has to be clear, simple, and, most of all, written in a language your readers are familiar with. There's much less chance they'll misunderstand what you say.

The leading brand of English for getting results is a natural, conversational style, the kind we all use when we talk. It's already streamlined for action, with short, familiar words.

You wouldn't, for example, talk like this: "Management is cognizant of the necessity of utilizing computer programs to facilitate the implementation of payroll procedures in order to bring about a reduction in clerical costs." Instead, you'd probably say, "We could save money if we did our payroll on computers." And the work would get done faster.

That's the main reason why pretentious phrasing and ten-dollar words, as impressive as they may seem, don't work in persuasive business writing. They don't sound familiar to the reader, who has to spend valuable time trying to figure out what you mean. Meanwhile, his response is slowed and your request is on hold.

Talk the reader's language. A conversational style puts you both on the same level immediately, winning acceptance from the reader because it's familiar, echoing the way he himself talks. In writing, a conversational style simulates a real-life conversation, as if you and the reader were already on friendly terms. Moreover, it ensures that *all* readers will understand your message as you intended it.

Although this clear style is basic to persuasion, your analysis of your readers will give you clues to other levels of language to use with special groups. If, for example, you're writing to a fellow chemist about a new experiment, go ahead and use the professional jargon you're both familiar with. It will create immediate acceptance and goodwill. But if you're presenting your findings to the board of directors, you should translate your scientific terminology so that the nonspecialist can understand it.

The perception is the reality for most people. Your readers will tend to react in terms of how they perceive your message. Language they can't understand is threatening; words they're familiar with seem friendlier. Because you want to be in charge of how your message is perceived, you should talk your reader's language.

The Gestalt factor in a message could also operate to give your reader a message you didn't intend. A school of psychologists gave the name Gestalt to a theory that says we all tend to perceive things in relation to the form, surroundings, or context in which they are presented. For example, a poorly typed or ungrammatical letter will surely give readers the impression that the writer is either incompetent or doesn't care, no matter how good the ideas presented.

The Gestalt factor in a message can also be used to advantage in persuasion. Politicians, for example, know the value of connecting themselves with such popular images as Mom, apple pie, and the American flag; the popularity rubs off on them.

In a similar and simple way, your echo of the reader's attitudes and language gives your message a positive feeling and gives you credibility.

Actually, to be sure your reader gets your message in the way you intend, the best thing you can do is to make it clear. The pretentious language of "officialese" creates a Gestalt that leaves too much room for the reader to interpret your message her own way.

Close the Credibility Gap

You may write a well-focused letter, but if your readers don't trust what you say, you'll never get to first base with them. A persuasive business writer must come across as a trustworthy and competent source of information. Credibility is improved when you demonstrate that you know what you are talking about, that you can back it up with evidence, and that you can explain it to readers in a language they understand.

Advertising uses testimonials to lend credibility. Tennis players are asked to endorse tennis balls, famous beauties to pitch perfume, and gourmet cooks to sell kitchen equipment. They have credibility.

The persuasion we find most credible, however, comes from someone we perceive as like ourselves. Aristotle advised: "Whatever quality the audience esteems, the speaker must attribute that quality to the object of his praise."[4] Thus, your echo of the reader will do most to enhance his belief in what you say.

Credibility is undermined by exaggeration, inflated language, clichés, and a hard sell. Understatement (and, it goes without saying, honesty) sells better. You want to make readers reach out for your ideas, not feel overwhelmed by them. An understated, factual approach makes room for the reader to participate and increases your credibility.

Television commercials that come on strong with fast talk and an avalanche of claims tend to arouse suspicion in an ever-more sophisticated audience of consumers. Buying should always seem to be a choice, not a coercion. For the most part, keep your "pitch" in a low key.

There are a few exceptions, however. Experiments with perception and attention span show that under some circumstances the more extreme your demand, the more action you are apt to get—that is, if you don't turn the reader off in the process.

Similarly, asking a high price, announcing a big bargain (but not cheapness), using an oversize picture or intense contrast or rapid movement can bring the attention-getting "just noticeable difference" (j.n.d.) factor into play. The theory is that to get twice as much attention, your picture or your message has to be four times bigger or smaller.[5] Crazy Eddie gets away with fast-talking commercials because the exaggeration is all in the speed of delivery; the ad may get more attention just because a listener must be more alert to catch what he is saying.

On occasion, you might want to bring these factors into play. Sales letters often need extra attention-getting devices like large headlines or graphics, for example. For the conservative business audience, however, the soft sell is more believable.

Play Up the Positive

To get people to remember your message, stress the positive side of things. People tend to block out and forget negatives. Assume a positive stance when you write. Say "I wish I could" instead of "I can't." Say "when" instead of "if."

Avoid blaming the reader. Rewrite sentences that say "You made a mistake" to "There is a mistake." Use general terms when the specific facts are negative: "We'd like to settle this matter," rather than "We'd like to settle your complaint about our incompetence."

Very few advertisements, you'll notice, mention negatives. Although sheer irritation value is said to have increased brand recognition for products like Wisk ("Ring around the collar"), advertisers know that the best way to get customers to say yes is to talk yes.

Find the positive side of your message, even when you have bad news. You'll put readers in a better frame of mind to accept and remember what you say.

Paint the Picture with Colorful Nouns and Active Verbs

The human brain responds more rapidly to an image than to a word, which is why a picture has always been worth a thousand words. It's also why persuasive writing uses language that conjures up for readers a vivid mental picture.

In your writing, the better you help readers visualize your concepts, the more persuasive you will be. You should use language that has built-in visual effects.

Words that call forth mental pictures are concrete and specific, like roses, blondes, Wall Street, red tape. Abstract, general words tend to remain purely theoretical. They don't create mental pictures: plant, human, financial community, bureaucracy.

Concrete language communicates—and persuades—because the words are linked to real things. They're sensuous words, referring to things people can see, taste, touch, smell, or hear. Abstract language refers to things that may exist only intellectually.

Language stands in for reality in a convenient way, as paper money does (or used to do) for gold. And, like money, language should have the kind of currency your readers can cash. You need words that translate into real experience for your reader.

Concrete, specific language—especially nouns—creates immediate understanding as it dramatizes your ideas in the reader's mind. Say "two weeks from today" instead of "soon." Talk "$100,000" instead of "substantial gain." Mention "our Atlanta headquarters" instead of "the facility."

Favor Nouns and Verbs in Persuasive Writing

Because they are the names for the people, places, things, and drama of the real world, nouns and verbs keep your writing anchored there, too. As Ernest Hemingway proved, you can write some pretty fascinating prose using mainly nouns and verbs. Adjectives tend to make everything float away. You should use them sparingly in persuasion. Would you buy a lawn mower that was billed as "Outstanding! Handy! Speedy!" or would you prefer one that "cuts grass in half the time with half the effort?"

Concrete language actually helps us to discriminate. It will make your message clear. And it will make what you say real to your readers.

Avoid Passive Verbs

Don't slow your sentences down by using passive verbs. Instead of saying "The work has been done," say who did it: "I did the work." The picture is sharper because the action is clear.

Active verbs energize your sentences and keep up the momentum of persuasion. Passive verbs tend to stall sentences and make them ambiguous.

Use Short Words, Short Sentences, and Short Paragraphs

The faster your readers understand, the more involved they'll get with your message, and the more receptive they will be. To make sure that your message comes across—that it gets read at all—make reading it easier.

Research by reading specialists like Rudolf Flesch and others has shown that short words, short sentences, and short paragraphs mean better comprehension. Flesch recommended that sentence length be kept between 17 and 22 words for optimum understanding.[6] Short paragraphs, shorter than the ones your English teacher said were acceptable back in high school, give readers the sense that your message is easy to read.

No matter what their educational level, people like to get information in the easiest way possible. Newspaper editors have always known this. Editors try to gauge the vocabulary they use to a level easy for their readers. *The New York Times,* for example, aims at about a twelfth-grade reader. Most television shows are pitched to sixth-grade levels, to make sure that no viewers are left out.

Unfortunately, many college textbooks use a vocabulary and sentence length that are actually way over the head of the average college senior. There are ways to gauge your own writing level. Using something called a Fog Index (Chapter Five), you can find out what the educational level of your writing is and how to raise or lower it.

None of this means that you have to downgrade your usual profundities to a kindergartener's level. On the contrary, a style streamlined to familiar words and short sentences is an expert way to connect with readers.

The Art of Persuasion

Persuasive language is "you-talk," not "I-talk" or "it-talk," as one good writer has put it.[7] Modern communication theory describes it in fancier terms: language is a code where persuasive language is "decoder-oriented," focused on and for the reader.

Either way, your readers are the key to your success in persuasion. Take good care of them.

Chapter Three

Three Formats
for Persuasion

Most messages in business writing have one of three functions:

1. To tell good news
2. To break bad news
3. To sell an idea or a product

Other functions, such as asking for payment, confirming a decision, or adjusting a claim, will fit into one of these three categories.

In all three categories, persuasion is a vital ingredient. Choose one of the following formats to instantly organize whatever message you write for maximum persuasion:

The Good News format, to tell good news
The Bad News format, to break bad news
The Sales, or AIM, format, to sell an idea or a product

Each of these formats is organized in a three- or four-paragraph structure designed to provide your message with an appropriate psychological order for persuasion. The last paragraph in each format has the same purpose: to call to action.

Form follows function. Add these formats to your repertoire and pull them out to match the purpose of your letter, memo, or sales piece.

Figure 3–1. The Good News format.

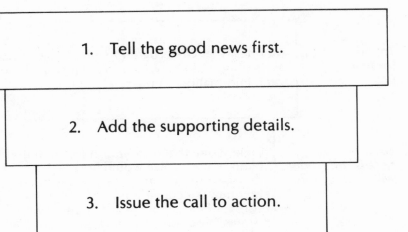

1. Tell the good news first.

2. Add the supporting details.

3. Issue the call to action.

In Chapter Six, practical applications for each of the three formats are illustrated in detail. But first, let's take a look at the structure of each format.

The Good News Format

If you have good news, tell the reader about it in your first paragraph. That's persuasive in itself. Positive news gets readers' attention and makes them receptive. It also helps them remember what you say.

The Good News format, Figure 3–1, borrows its inverted pyramid shape from journalism, where the first sentence of a news story must summarize the major news point. As its name implies, the inverted pyramid format puts the "biggest," or most important, point at the top.

The main point of your letter or memo will be up front, too, to satisfy the reader's natural curiosity: What's this about? And the sooner a reader understands your main point, the better she will understand your entire message.

Use the Good News format to organize most business writing, except when you have bad or disappointing news. Then it's better to build up to your main point and prepare the reader.

Figure 3–2.   An example using the Good News format.

Tells the reason for writing first

Your new speech-recognition telephones sound fascinating, and I'm writing to ask if you'll send us some information on them.

Supplies the details the reader will need to reply

A telephone that dials your number at the sound of your voice would be a real laborsaver in our offices, especially in our eight new executive suites. We're in the process of installing the communication systems in our new building, and we'd like to know what your telephones could do for us and what they would cost.

Issues a call to action

I'd appreciate hearing from you as soon as possible, so that I can present the idea to the chairman before he decides on something else.

The second, or middle, paragraph of the Good News format should explain your main point and offer the supporting details that will help your reader understand the message.

The call to action in the third, and last, paragraph suggests what you'd like the reader to do. Since the end of a letter is the most emphatic position, that's where you spell out the action you want the reader to take.

Figure 3–2 provides an example of how you would use the Good News format in writing a business inquiry.

Figure 3–3. The Bad News format.

Y stands for you.
Express understanding of the reader by sympathizing with his concerns.

E stands for explain.
Give whatever details the reader will need to understand the bad news that follows.

S stands for state.
Tell the bad news.

Call to action.
Don't repeat the bad news. Instead, suggest an appropriate response or action for the reader to take, or switch the subject to a bit of resale.

The Bad News, or YES, Format

Business writing involves just as much no as yes. But saying no has a tendency to put your readers on the defensive, especially if you say it first. They won't be inclined to read the rest of your letter or to accept your turndown with goodwill.

Psychologically, readers will be more receptive to bad or disappointing news if it is presented *after* you've prepared them for it.

The Bad News format is a four-paragraph format designed to break the news in a straightforward, informative way, but first it prepares the reader to accept it. The rule in using this format is: *Never break the bad news first.*

You can use the YES acronym to help you remember the first three parts of the Bad News format. (The fourth and last part, as always, is the call to action.) Figure 3–3 shows the structure of the four-paragraph Bad News format.

Y *stands for you.* In the first paragraph, express your understanding of the reader by echoing his concerns. Show that you understand his problem, sympathize with any inconvenience, recognize the difficulties he faces. Connect with the reader as soon as possible. If there is some good news, start with that, or give the bad news a positive slant. Even if the order has been delayed two weeks, you can still say: *Your order will be on its way March 14.*

E *stands for explain.* In the second paragraph, lead up to the bad or disappointing news by offering the explanation for it first, complete with any details the reader may need to understand it: *The wildcat strike this month delayed all our shipments.*

S *stands for state.* The third paragraph states the bad news: *"We're upset, too, that your order is still sitting on the dock in Detroit."* Because the reader already knows the reason for the bad news, it's a little easier to take. The third paragraph is a good place to offer your apologies, but don't overdo it.

Call to action. In the Bad News format, you can use the call to action for several purposes:

- To tell the reader what to do in response to your letter
- To close on a positive note
- To switch the subject entirely, perhaps with a bit of resale: *As one of our good customers, you'll be receiving an advance sample this week of our newest product, to be introduced next spring. We'd like to hear what you think of it.*
- Remember, in the call to action *never* repeat the bad news.

In the memo in Figure 3–4, the Bad News format is used to advantage in a threatening situation.

The AIM Format

The AIM format is designed specifically for selling, and can strengthen the persuasion in anything you write. Use it to ask for money, collect a debt, promote a plan, convince your reader, or sell a product or service.

In business, you're often writing to people who are on overload, in a deluge of information that keeps us all drowning in paperwork. Shown in Figure 3–5, the AIM format is designed for the busy reader; it is

(continued on p. 40)

Figure 3–4.   An example using the Bad News format.

Heads off reader resistance with understanding and praise	Everyone has been extremely cooperative under the pressure of our stepped-up work load, and I've been very happy about the way you've all pitched in at a tough time.
Builds up to the bad news by providing background to cushion the blow	Times are still tough, with interest rates on the rise again and competition from imports. When the new legislation goes through later this year, we should start to show better profits. Then we're going to talk about some adjustments in salary and benefit schedules.
Surrounds bad news with concern and shared feelings	But for the next six months, we're all going to have to do some belt-tightening to prevent any layoffs or shutdowns. We'd like to avoid it, but it looks as if a temporary wage and salary freeze, effective May 1, is the only fair alternative. The other options—losing jobs, closing the door—are even less attractive.
Switches the subject, ends on the upbeat	Again, thank you all for the effort you've been putting in, which now appears to be on the verge of paying off. The advance orders we've started receiving on our forthcoming product suggest that a strong turnaround should begin by the end of this year. Let's keep working together to make that hope a reality.

Figure 3–5.   The AIM format.

A stands for attention.

Use a "grabber":
  Make a promise.
  Tell a story.
  Ask a question.
  Arouse curiosity.
  Tell the news.

I stands for interest.

Describe the product or idea in terms of benefits
  for the reader.
Dramatize it; sell use.

M stands for motivation.

Cite statistics, testimonials, warranties, guarantees; offer solid evidence that what you say is
  true.

Call to action.

Make it easy.
Make it urgent.
Make it rewarding.

---

planned in a sequence of steps for attention, interest, motivation, and decision, closely following the stages of buyer behavior.

   A stands for attention. In your opening paragraph, capture your reader's attention by using one of the "grabbers" discussed below.
   Make a promise. In your first sentence, offer readers an incentive by

stressing the benefits of the action you want them to take: *We can make sure you never have to wait for parts again, with our new overnight delivery service,* or *You could be a millionaire by this time next year.*

Tell a story. Narratives are a natural for getting readers involved. They'll usually finish the story because they want to find out what happened. By that time, they're into your letter and will go ahead and finish that too:

> When the Smiths heard about our new investment service, they came in to find out what it was all about. John and Mary Smith decided to shift some of their funds into a stock we'd recommended, and today they're saying it was the best advice they've ever had.

Arouse curiosity. Slogans like "Please don't squeeze the Charmin" that arouse curiosity have moved lots of products. Get the reader to read on: *You can cut your telephone bills by 30 percent in the next five minutes.*

Ask a question. Questions set up an involuntary reaction: readers feel compelled to answer. Just be sure that your question can't be answered no: *When was the last time you saw Paris?*

Tell the news. As in the Good News format, start off by telling the reader what she's been waiting to hear: *We've repaired your hair dryer and it's ready to be picked up.*

Announce a breakthrough. Breakthroughs always get attention: *We've found a cure for the common cold.* Other grabbers: Mention the reader's name; offer a bargain price or a money-back free trial; use a quotation or a pun.

I *stands for interest.* Build interest by describing your product in detail. Talk benefits. Dramatize it as part of the reader's life. Play up the Central Selling Point:

> Our new parts-inventory system means you'll never be out of luck, waiting for the parts you need. We're *never* out, and we'll deliver 24 hours a day.

M *stands for motivation.* Use the third paragraph of the AIM format to offer solid evidence for what you say. Cite statistics, quote testimonials, offer guarantees, mention the warranty:

> Vice President John Jones had this to say about our service: *Your timing is superb. We've been able to meet our spring production schedule for the first year, thanks to your fast delivery.*

Figure 3–6. An example using the AIM format.

Captures attention by "telling the news"	The position you advertised in Sunday's *Times* sounds like just what I've been waiting for. I'm a seasoned, degreed self-starter who'd like to work as a project analyst for Citicorp.
Describes the "product" in terms of reader benefits	My five years as a financial control manager with Touche Ross and my M.B.A. from Harvard mean you'd be hiring a project analyst with demonstrated ability.
Gives factual evidence to support the claims	My experience includes price and cost analysis, long-range capital requirement projections, and high-visibility work with all levels of financial management.
Issues a call to action	I'm ready for the challenge of a senior management position that will give me a chance to supervise a professional staff, and I'd like to talk to you about the possibilities of a career at Citicorp, at your convenience.

Call to action. Everything in the AIM format is designed for this moment of decision, the call to action. In the last paragraph, spell out the action you want. Inconclusive letters tend not to get answered.

Make action easy and simple. Make it urgent. And make it rewarding.

- To move the reader out of his natural inertia, give him something to do: a toll-free number to call or a reply card to return. Or ask him to verify the date for the meeting.
- Add a sense of urgency: a deadline or date when the offer ends or when it will be too late to act.
- Add benefits: remind the reader of what's in it for him:

You can start right now to eliminate costly holdups. Give me a call at 555–5678. By the end of the week, we can have you set up in a made-to-order delivery plan that will begin as soon as you say so.

The cover letter in Figure 3–6 is a good example of the versatility of the AIM format.

Form Follows Function

As you use these three formats, you can develop your own variations, tailoring them to reach special readers and fit different situations. In writing a collection letter, for example, you may find that the Bad News format works better for you than the AIM format. Or that the Good News format is best for writing memos because it gets right to the point.

Here are some additional points to consider:

- When your reader is friendly and likely to agree with you, use the Good News format to present the viewpoint you share with the reader and get him on your side right away.
- When the reader is already highly involved and interested in your subject, use the AIM format to build expectations and then strengthen your mutual agreement conclusively.
- When your reader is unfriendly and likely to disagree, use the Bad News format. Present the side he agrees with first. Work up to your own views in the third paragraph.
- When the reader is indifferent or disinterested, use the AIM format to get attention. Echo the reader, showing how your viewpoint is like his.

Chapter Four

The Creative Connection

The notion of creativity in business writing may seem a paradox. Routine language and routine methods—"that's the way we've always done it"—are easier. Yet, it's clear that tired language and traditional methods don't work in persuasion.

Persuasive writing needs new ideas and fresh language to engage busy readers and build motivation. You'll need to tap into your innate creativity to snap readers out of their natural inertia and resistance to change.

The following are some techniques for generating ideas, improving creativity, beating procrastination, and overcoming writer's block.

The Creative Process

New studies show that the most successful executives have developed a "multidimensional" style of thinking.[1] This has less to do with IQ than with creativity, with the ability to be flexible and to grasp connections among rapidly changing events. Instead of being locked into a rigid approach, these executives have learned to experiment and to entertain new ideas.

Creativity isn't limited to the geniuses of the world. Psychologists say that most adults use only 10 percent of the creative capacity they were born with. In the structured atmosphere of school and business, and in the effort to "do it right," the creativity we had as children gets lost. The good news is that we can tap back into it.

Creativity is a process that has four distinct phases: preparation, incubation, inspiration, and verification. Artists, inventors, and musicians go through these phases, too. For the most part, their inspiration comes after preparation and hard work. And, like children at play, they're willing to entertain some notions that may have seemed pretty silly at first.

Preparation

In the same way that you'd feed data into a computer to get it working, you must prime your mind for creativity. Gather all the information you need to understand your subject. Immerse yourself in this material. Get to know it from every angle.

The "Know your customer" and "Know your product" steps in Copythink are designed to help you collect all the data you need before you write. "Ideas come from the unconscious," as David Ogilvy observes, "but [it] has to be well-informed." [2]

Incubation

Psychologists say that the second phase of creativity—letting go of the whole thing—is crucial. Once you've prepared and primed your mind, give yourself a break from thinking about your subject. Creativity is a matter of allowing your brain to do some of the work on its own. Amazingly, it does, if you let it. Artistic people have often testified to the value of letting their ideas "incubate."

Meanwhile, as you're going about your business, your mind is making new combinations of the ingredients you've fed it. You've probably experienced a sudden rush of ideas just when you least expected it—in the shower, in a traffic jam, in the middle of the night. When you quit working so hard on a problem, the solution you've been looking for suddenly comes.

Allow time for this to happen. Exercise, coffee breaks, even a nap during your workday can help this stage along. Thinking improves when you're lying down, which may be why Thomas Edison kept a cot in his laboratory. To get your mind into its creative mode, you have to work it hard for a spell, then let things marinate.

Inspiration

Not every inspiration comes like a bolt out of the blue. It may be a commonsense solution that comes after careful weighing of all the possibilities. But there are things you can do to encourage inspiration.

Get rid of negative thoughts. Banish "I can't do this," or "That's a stupid idea," or "I'll never get this done in time." Clear roadblocks like these out of your mind to pave the way for new ideas.

Reject nothing. Do some brainstorming. The more ideas you generate, the more chance that one of them will be really new and workable.

Write down everything that occurs to you. The brain functions best visually. Your list of ideas will give you something to look over, edit, and consider.

Verification

You can let your inner critic have full sway at the verification stage. This is the test-market phase, a time to evaluate and revise. But it's important that you delay evaluation until you've worked through the first three phases. Otherwise, you'll nip creativity in the bud.

Examine your ideas for flaws and work the kinks out of them. Test their reality quotient by telling someone else about them. Get some distance; let everything cool off again one more time.

Creativity and Persuasive Writing

At each step in persuasion, getting some creative play in your thinking will help. Novelty helps break through readers' natural resistance.

You need imagination to understand your readers and their needs. You want to find the best way to motivate them. And you want to find a compelling Central Selling Point, one that's new and fresh. Your call to action should be inventive enough to generate the response you want.

In writing, your creativity will help you find vivid and engaging ways to phrase your message and break out of the routine. Fresh language makes your ideas look newer and attracts readers. Egg-O-Mania, in Figure 4–1, is an example of how creative thinking can transform an everyday object.

Figure 4–1. Egg-o-mania (by Bob Pliskin).

Whoever hatched up the egg was indeed a Great Creator, but he didn't know the first thing about packaging.

One look at the egg will tell you he believed—like all package designers and manufacturers—that packages are designed for products.

Well, that's scrambled thinking. Packages really should be designed for consumers. Of course, the package must preserve and protect its product. But ideally, packaging is positioning. A great package positions and promotes its product to a specific, targeted consumer segment.

Now let's take a hard-boiled look at the sad and sorry package that is the egg.

 Eggs won't stand up by themselves. They roll too easily.

 They break.

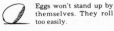 They require special packaging.

 Eggs are segregated.

 But the egg is a "me-too" package.

 And a blind purchase.

 Eggs contain chicks...

They get squeezed into milk-bottles by high-school freshmen.

...or alligators.

All in all, eggs have a thoroughly bad image. Eggs are obsolete, marketing-wise.

We can forgive the Great Creator His mistake. After all, Modern Marketing Research didn't exist back then. Segmentation studies and delta matrices and multi-dimensional perceptual mapping hadn't been invented. It's no wonder the egg is not the package it's cracked up to be. But put *today's* top package designers to work, and look what happens to the old-fashioned egg!

We get specialized eggs, positioned for specific target markets.

  In other words, market segmented eggs.

Consider the possibilities! Convenient eggs for today's fast-packed life styles...

 A flip-top egg.

 A zip-taped egg.

 A perforated egg that opens easily.

 The automatic egg...

 ...and the semi-automatic egg.

 A self-timing egg.

The zippered egg—easy to open and easy to close.

What about eggs for technology buffs:

A programed egg.

 Impact plastic, transparent eggshelled eggs.

And eggs for trend-setters:

 An altogether All-New Egg.

 And the aerosol-spray egg...

 The more visible egg...

 And the insulated egg.

And don't forget eggs for the budget-watcher:

 A price-marked egg...

 The U.P.C. egg...

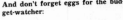 Marked eggs—Small, Medium and Large...

 ...and eggs you can buy by the yard.

How about eggs for the space-saver:

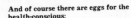 A stand-up egg.

 A stand-up egg that stacks on shelves.

 Like this.

 A faceted egg that can't roll easily.

And of course there are eggs for the health-conscious:

 The all-natural egg—no preservatives, of course.

 The measure-your-calories squeeze-bottle egg.

 And long, thin, low-cholesterol, easy-to-lay eggs.

 And last but not least, for egg-o-maniacs: New, transparent, faceted, stackable, soluble, unbreakable, zip-top eggs.

Now *that's* great packaging in an egg-shell.#

Mr. Pliskin, president and creative director of The First Team Inc., New York-based new-products development company, was egged on by the editors to hatch this article.

Writer's Block and Other Ailments

By putting the creative process to work for you, you can take writing out of the discouraging framework past experience may have built. You'll stop thinking of writing as a chore and start seeing it as a strategic tool.

Writing is hard work, no question. Dry spells and difficulty getting started haunt every writer. But you can learn to work around or through them. The following are some ideas for doing that.

Hints for Getting Started

The most difficult part of writing, for most people, is just getting started. Here are some ways to help make it easier:

Create time and space for writing. You may not be making room for writing in your workday. Decide what time of day suits you best for writing. Firmly block off that time in your schedule. Shut the door to your office, keep yourself focused, and write—even if for just 15 minutes at the start.

The more writing becomes a part of your life, the easier it will be. Professionals write every day for a certain amount of time, whether they get through a whole chapter or just one sentence. That's how Ernest Hemingway wrote.

Talk it out. Most of us find it easier to talk than to write. Use that facility to advantage. Talk into a tape recorder. Many writers, including Norman Mailer and Studs Terkel, have written entire books that way. The only problem is that you have to transcribe and edit the tape afterwards.

Keep notepads handy. Ideas surface when you least expect them. Keep paper handy and jot them down so that you won't lose them.

Try free writing. Free writing is "free" because you can put down your thoughts in any order, without criticism. Even if you just write, "I'm sitting here trying to write and I can't think of anything to say," you've started. Other sentences won't be far behind. Free writing also helps you squelch your inner critic, the one who's always warning, "This better be good."

Brainstorm. You can brainstorm at any point in the creative process to generate ideas. But you'll find brainstorming most productive after you've done your homework. Get rid of negative thoughts. Reject nothing.

Marinate. Schedule time during a writing assignment for walking around, staring out the window, even taking a nap. These brief letting-go periods improve creativity.

Editing Checklist

All good writers revise. In the evaluation phase of writing, you can probably improve on what you've written by doing some editing.

Here's a checklist of things to look for in editing your own work or the work of others:

- *Read it out loud.* Would you actually talk that way? If not, the style may be stilted or unnatural. For all but the most formal business writing, a conversational style is appropriate and will put your reader at ease.
- *Check your vocabulary.* Use specific, concrete nouns and active verbs. Get rid of language that's vague or overly abstract.
- *Eliminate the passive voice wherever possible.* Use the active voice instead ("I noticed" instead of "It has been noticed").
- *Cut copy.* Get rid of extra words, cut sentences to 17 to 22 words. Paragraph more frequently.
- *Make sure that you've said what you thought you were saying.* Check your scratch outline. Use one of the persuasive formats to organize the message.
- *Add headings to improve readability.* Use lists to make points stand out.
- *Give sentences a yes flavor by taking out the no.* A negative slant turns off the reader.
- *Check for errors in spelling and grammar and for typos.* Strive to make your writing letter-perfect. Having a sharp-eyed colleague scan your work may help (you can do the same for her). If you're too close to the writing, it's easy to overlook even the most obvious howlers.

The Writer as Merchant

It will help if you can develop something of a merchant's mentality. As a persuasive writer, you'll also understand what you're doing better if you can draw on your own experience as a consumer.

Do a little creative research in the field; watch what goes on when people buy and sell. When you go to the supermarket or stroll the aisles of a department store, pay attention to the come-ons and to your reactions. What makes you want to buy? Why does one brand of cereal or soap appeal to you more than others? Take your mental and emotional pulse as you shop; it will teach you something about buyer behavior.

Who Can Be Persuaded?

Recognize that your most educated customers will not necessarily be the most resistant. Paradoxically, the more mental flexibility a reader has, the more susceptible he may be to persuasive tactics, even though he will also be more critical. Well-educated people are more easily convinced by subtle verbal argument. Street smarts can go a long way in resisting the hard sell. The uneducated reader is less likely to be reading, first of all, and has an innate suspicion of people who can throw words around.[3]

There is evidence that, because of upbringing and cultural expectations, women have been more conditioned to give in. That may no longer hold. Consider too that women, as the people who make most of the buying decisions for families, are very savvy customers.[4]

Wives have always known, for example, that the best time to ask husbands for something is when they're in a "food condition," a behavioral term for that satisfied state that makes a business lunch a prime time to get things done. People remember better and are more responsive if they read or hear something while they're eating. The advertising on the back of the cereal box is there for a reason.[5]

Research shows we are at our most persuadable when we are anxious or have low self-esteem, though these two factors can also serve to make us misinterpret a message. We are more inclined to be led when we lack confidence or are worried.

People also tend to make an "assimilation error" that can be used to advantage in persuasion. If your readers perceive your message to be close to their own viewpoint, they are more inclined to assimilate it—and interpret it to be even closer than it actually is.

This can boomerang, however. If readers discover discrepancies or conflicts, they will be much more likely to reject the message out of hand. We have a "latitude of acceptance," a kind of grid that filters reality according to our own beliefs and values.[6] People are more likely to listen and respond to suggestions they already agree with, and more likely to avoid those they don't favor.

The reader's perception of where you stand is central to the acceptance of your message. The nearer you are to that reader's familiar territory, the better. Right or wrong, a persuader cast in the reader's image will be the most effective.

Chapter Five

The Style of Persuasion

Words are persuasive only when people understand them. Where time is money, it makes sense to use language that your readers can cash on the spot. The faster they understand your message, the faster your persuasive strategies will take effect. That's why your writing style—the medium through which your message flows—is important.

Talk the Reader's Language

The best style for persuasion is usually the one your reader already uses: the conversational style. It's ideal for persuasion because it's familiar: it echoes the way the reader himself talks. He can understand your message immediately and without effort.

The conversational style is clear, brief, specific, natural, and positive. (See Figure 5–1.) If you can write in the same kind of up-close, everyday language you use in person, your style will meet all these criteria.

The outdated business jargon in Figure 5–2 is cumbersome and obscure. Use familiar, everyday language to persuade, instead of such outmoded phrasing.

Figure 5–1. Talk the reader's language.

Keep It Simple

Strike three.
Get your hand off my knee.
You're overdrawn.
Your horse won.
Yes.
No.
You have the account.
Walk.
Don't walk.
Mother's dead.
Basic events
require simple language.
Idiosyncratically euphuistic
eccentricities are the
promulgators of
triturable obfuscation.
What did you do last night?
Enter into a meaningful
romantic involvement
or
fall in love?
What did you have for
breakfast this morning?
The upper part of a hog's
hind leg with two oval
bodies encased in a shell
laid by a female bird
or
ham and eggs?
David Belasco, the great
American theatrical producer,
once said, "If you can't
write your idea on the
back of my calling
card,
you don't have a clear idea."

How we perform as individuals will determine
how we perform as a nation. FREE: If you would like
an 8½" × 11" reprint of this message, write to
Harry J. Gray, Chairman and Chief Executive Officer,
United Technologies, Box 360, Hartford, CT 06141

Reprinted by permission of United Technologies.

Figure 5–2.   Everyday substitutes for business jargon.

Instead of:	*Write:*
As per	According to
At this writing	Now
Attached herewith	Attached
Despite the fact that	Although
Due to the fact that	Because
Enclosed please find	Here is
In connection with	About
It has come to my attention	(Avoid this delaying action; get to the point.)
Pursuant to your request	As you asked
We are in receipt of	We received
With reference to	About
Yours of the 25th	Your letter

Streamline Your Style

You can achieve a conversational tone in your writing through streamlining. Keep in mind that the most memorable phrases are short and simple:

> Give me liberty or give me death.
> Play it again, Sam.
> Winning isn't everything; it's the only thing.
> Less is more.

Simple words and short statements are clear and easy to remember. There's less chance that a reader will misinterpret their meaning.

You don't have to oversimplify your writing to grade-school level. There is plenty of use for the rich and varied words the English language provides—*if* they're getting your message across. But you want your reader to remember what you say. So write to express, not to impress.

There's a great deal of elegance—in the mathematical sense of being precise—in simplicity. Elegance in writing is refusal: the refusal to say too much, ramble on too long, use too many difficult words, or bore the reader.

It's not easy to streamline your writing style. It would be easier just to go on and on. The basic style we're advocating here may mean that you'll have to put your own style on a diet. But losing weight—the weight of big words and long sentences—will give your writing more energy. It will have the verbal fitness to go the distance in persuasion. Here are five ways to streamline your style:

1. Be clear. Use plain English. Never use long words when short ones will do. Tailor your vocabulary to your reader so that there will be no misunderstanding.
2. Be brief. Go for the fast read and the pared-down sentence. Use short words, short sentences, and short paragraphs. A well-edited message pays off in reader understanding.
3. Be specific. Use real-world words—concrete nouns and active verbs—to give readers a picture. Say "$300 a week" instead of "remuneration." Talk about living to the age of 85 instead of "health," about owning a Rolls-Royce instead of "wealth," or about "two weeks with pay" instead of "vacation."
4. Be natural. Write it the way you'd say it in person. Strive for the friendly and informal. Use contractions, just as you'd do in conversation. Say "I" or "we" instead of the impersonal "one" or "the company." (But don't be too chatty or personal.)
5. Be positive. A positive approach creates the proper climate for persuasion. Readers like to associate with the positive. And it takes you less time and space to say yes than to explain why you are saying no.

Let's take a closer look at each of these five principles.

Be Clear

If customers are suspicious of salespeople who talk too much (and they usually are) they'll be especially wary of writing that is wordy, difficult, or takes too much time to understand. To persuade, you must be clear. The word *clear* means "easily grasped," "distinct," "free from confusion." Clarity begins in language that readers feel at home with. Know your customer. If you talk your reader's language, you'll increase the chances that she'll get the meaning you intend.

Would you say, "Conformity to a standard of behavior which stresses integrity has the optimum probability of producing satisfactory end results"? Or would you say, "Honesty is the best policy"?

For some reason, when we write we stiffen up and bolster our position with hard-to-understand words and ponderous sentences. To streamline your style, you have to go back to basics, to plain English.

Figure 5–3.   Short words for long.

Instead of:	*Write:*
At this point in time	Now
For the purpose of	For
Impacted	Affected
In close proximity	Near
In the event that	If
Momentarily	Soon (*Momentarily* means "just for a moment.")
Remuneration	Pay
Respectively	Each
Terminated	Fired
Thanking you in advance	(Never say this—omit.)
The question as to whether	If
The reason is because	Because
Utilize	Use

For example, instead of "consequently," say "so." Instead of "in the manner in which," say "how." Instead of "utilize," say "use." Never use a long word when a short word will do. In Figure 5–3, you'll find other words and phrases to avoid, and short and simple words to use instead.

Our Anglo-Saxon heritage of single-syllable words offers plenty of ways to say what we mean. After all, that's where we got all those four-letter words we find so emphatic.

Make your language user-friendly. In New York City, someone has gotten through to officialdom about using clear, familiar language on street signs: "Don't even *think* of parking here"; "Littering is messy and dirty, so don't do it." In user-friendly English, these signs get a lot more attention than did the traditional "No Parking" and "No Littering" signs they replaced.

Clarify Your Sentences

For clarity's sake, stick to standard English word order in your sentences. The subject-verb-object order (S-V-O) is native to English syntax. It is easiest for people to read and grasp because it is so familiar:

$$S \quad V \quad O$$
John wrote the book.

Newspapers rely on the S-V-O order for a fast read in headlines and news stories. And you can use it to clarify your sentences. Your readers will understand faster when you use the word order that's already in their heads. Say "We discovered an error" rather than "It was discovered recently that an error was made."

The S-V-O pattern can be varied by adding clauses, phrases, or modifiers in the "free space" before, after, or between the three basic components:

S   *V*   *O*   *modifying phrase*

John wrote the book on leveraged buy-outs.

modifier   *S*   *V*   *O*   *clausal modifier*

My colleague John wrote the new book he sent me.

A second basic pattern, or word order, is subject-verb-complement, or S-V-C:

S   *V*   *C*

We are Americans.

In this sentence, the third element, the complement, refers back to the subject. The S-V-C pattern results when you use a linking verb, such as *be, am, is, are, was, were, been, seem, feel, look,* or *smell.* Here action is muted into a state of being or reacting. Although such sentences are necessary to expression, they should be used sparingly in persuasive writing. Overuse of linking verbs saps prose of its vitality and makes it stolid.

Based on the S-V-O or S-V-C pattern, two or more sentences can be combined to produce patterns called compound, complex, and compound-complex sentences:

1. S-V-O or simple sentence:

   Betty sold the company.
2. Compound sentence:

   Betty sold the company and she bought a farm.
   (Two simple sentences combined)
3. Complex sentence:

   When Betty sold the company, she bought a farm.
   (One simple sentence and a dependent clause)
4. Compound-complex sentence:

When Betty sold the company, she bought a farm; it gave her something to do, she said.
(Compound sentence with a dependent clause)

Write Persuasive Sentences

A good persuasive writing style should be varied, using all four kinds of sentence design to speed up, slow down, and modulate the flow of thought. The ability to write good sentences—complete ones that give the reader the right signals—reflects the quality of your thinking. Writing *is* thinking. And the sentence is the basic unit of thought in writing.

Indeed, the sentence is defined as a complete thought. That means it has a subject (an actor) and a predicate (an action and a receiver of that action), a who-did-what-to-whom chain of events that vitalizes the meaning of the sentence.

A poet once described the English sentence as an electric circuit charged with meaning. If your sentences are put together well, their charge of meaning connects with the reader, who can plug in to the direct current of your thoughts. Persuasive writing needs sentences that convey this kind of charge.

Your sentences themselves can be effective tools for the trade of persuasion when they are clear, easy to read, and constructed to emphasize the most important points. Let's take a look at some ways to make your sentences work persuasively.

Use sentence design for emphasis. The beginnings and endings of sentences speak the most emphatically. Your placement of word groups, choice of words, length of sentence, and ranking of its clauses will all help to emphasize important ideas.

Placement. Put the main words or ideas first, in an emphatic S-V-O pattern; choose your words carefully for these major elements.

Or end your sentence with the main clause, that is, the main S-V-O construction. Trial lawyers have perfected the art of the periodic sentence, in which the main clause of the entire statement isn't completed until the final word. It's good for summations and for keeping juries at attention.

Since my client was out of the country at the time, attending to business and vacationing with his two young children, he could not have committed this crime.

Word choice. To emphasize, use specific language: *Poor people, even in America, often go hungry.* To de-emphasize, cast the statement into general, abstract language: *Some of the disadvantaged may have difficulty in attaining required nutritional levels.*

Sentence length. Vary the lengths of your sentences to avoid monotony and give your writing vitality. Use a very short sentence occasionally to give drama to your prose: *"The plan succeeded."* You can even use a fragment, deliberately, to emphasize: *"And none too soon."*

Ranking of ideas. Subordinate ideas to sort them out for the reader, to emphasize, or to underplay:

> *subordinate*　　　*main clause*
> If you get lemons,　make lemonade.

A list can be especially attention-getting and also helps organize and rank your ideas.

Copythink has three steps:

1. Know your customer.
2. Know your product.
3. Find the Central Selling Point.

Use Parallelism

The classical art of rhetoric had its roots in public speaking, where the audience couldn't go back and read what had been said or hold it in mind very long. Parallel structures in the speaker's sentences helped audiences to retain and understand a speech.

It's still good advice to use parallelism, both for oratory and for the written word. Recall President John F. Kennedy's famous phrasing:

> Ask not what your country can do for you,
> but what you can do for your country.

By lining up your ideas in similar word order and repeating phrases, you can organize your message in a way that's particularly easy for a reader to understand. The signals are built into the sentence structure, are repeated, and provide a framework for your thoughts.

In persuasive writing, such patterns tend to create a formal tone. Use them sparingly, and only for major statements or points that you'd like the reader to remember. Parallelism is useful, too, in giving unity to a list of ideas or to the subheadings in a memo or sales letter.

Three basic sentence problems. There are three common sentence errors that indicate that the writer hasn't thought through the message. The first is the *sentence fragment,* which consists of an incomplete thought punctuated as if it were a bona fide sentence. Here are some examples:

> Although we requested delivery last week.
> Being of sound mind.
> Like a man without a country.

These are sentence fragments because their meaning—their thought—is incomplete, either because of a word ("Although," in the first sentence), a verb in a nonactive, participial form ("being"), or lack of a verb.

Revised, these fragments become sentences:

> The shipment is 10 days late although we requested delivery last
> week.
> *(To correct a fragment, add it to an existing sentence.)*

> I am of sound mind.
> *(To correct a fragment, put the verb in active form.)*

> He felt like a man without a country.
> *(To correct a fragment, give it a subject and a verb.)*

Sentence fragments can, however, be useful for emphasis when used deliberately. Here, for instance, they create a sense of anticipation:

> Now.
> The car you've been waiting for.
> Fireball II.
> The car that's hot today.

This machine-gun effect should be used sparingly.

The second basic problem is the *comma splice.* This punctuation error results from joining, or splicing, two complete sentences together with an inadequate "glue," the comma. The comma is the signal for a pause, not for a full stop like the period or a real slowdown like the semicolon.

Wrong: The order went through, the company lost track of it.

There are several ways to correct a comma splice:

1. Use the semicolon to join two complete sentences that are closely related in meaning:
    The order went through; the company lost track of it.
2. Keep the comma, and add extra "glue", a coordinating conjunction like *and* or *but:*
    The order went through, but the company lost track of it.
3. Use a period to separate the sentences entirely:
    The order went through. The company lost track of it.

When sentences are very closely related, it's good writing to join them with a semicolon for easy reading. In our comma splice, the best solution is No. 2, which preserves the association but conveys a special meaning.

A third basic sentence problem is the *run-on sentence*. This is another punctuation error. As opposed to the sentence fragment, which stops too soon, the run-on sentence never knows *when* to stop. There's no punctuation to indicate where one complete thought ends and another begins:

The order went through the company lost track of it.

The sentence has all the right ingredients but requires proper punctuation:

A semicolon to show the separate entities of meaning, *or*
A coordinating conjunction and a comma, *or*
A period, dividing it up into two sentences

Be Brief

Short words, short sentences, and short paragraphs make reading easy. Be brief. People have a resistance to reading. They like to get information in the easiest way possible, which explains the broad appeal of television and radio: it takes less effort to watch television or listen to the radio than to read.

That's your challenge in an audiovisual age: to lower the reader's resistance to reading by making your writing look fast and easy to read.

Research has shown that sentences between 17 and 22 words long help make reading fast and easy. Design yours to meet that standard. If you tend to write long, clause-ridden sentences, use the divide-and-conquer method. Cut them in half, using just one idea.

The Divide-and-Conquer Method

Here's a sentence that could use help:

It has been brought to our attention that in the introduction of our new consumer personal computer reference manual, an inadvertent error was made that resulted in misinformation about problem determination procedures that appear in operation section 4–1 under "Checking Electrical Cables."

Divide it in half:

It has been brought to our attention that in the introduction of our new consumer personal computer reference manual, an inadvertent error was made . . .

. . . that resulted in misinformation about problem determination procedures that appear in operation section 4–1 under "Checking Electrical Cables."

Conquer—make two complete sentences out of the original:

It has been brought to our attention that in the introduction of our new consumer personal computer reference manual, an inadvertent error was made.

This resulted in misinformation about problem determination procedures that appear in operation section 4–1 under "Checking Electrical Cables."

Then work to make both sentences clearer:

We've just discovered an error in the new personal computer manual you received recently. We'd like to correct a typo in section 4–1, "Checking Electrical Cables," so you won't have any problem connecting your computer.

Use Frequent Paragraphs

Break your text into readable pieces and leave attractive white space. Try for three or four sentences per paragraph. Each paragraph should center on a single main idea. When the idea changes, start a new paragraph.

A one-sentence paragraph can be very emphatic when you want an idea to stand out.

Avoid Wordiness

Look for ways to get one word to do the work of two. Don't say, *"In the matter of your recent order, the company was informed that our supplier cannot make delivery for two weeks.*" Just tell the customer, "*Your order will arrive two weeks from Monday.*"

Get rid of excess baggage. Cut fillers like "at this point in time" to "now." Say "near" instead of "in close proximity." You'll lose nothing in the translation but needless words. In persuasive writing, less is more.

Find Your Fog Index

A simple formula devised by a writing consultant can help you find out whether your writing is clear and brief enough for your readers.[1] This formula, aptly named the Fog Index, measures the length of your sentences and the proportion of "hard," or multisyllable, words you're using. The results will tell you how easy or hard your writing is to read and will help you clarify your style. Here is the procedure:

1. Take a 100-word sample of your writing (to get complete sentences, you can go over the limit by a few words). Try to choose a sample that's typical of your everyday business writing.
2. Count the number of complete sentences in your sample. Now, divide that number into the total word count of the passage. This gives you the average sentence length in your sample.
3. Next, count the number of words of three (or more) syllables in the sample. Do not count: 1) proper names; 2) verbs with -*ed*, -*es*, or -*ing* endings that make them three syllables; or 3) words compounded of simpler words, like "nevertheless" or "newspaper."
4. Divide the total number of words in your sample into the total number of "hard" words in order to get the percentage of "hard" words in the passage.
5. Last, add the average sentence length to the percentage of hard words. Then multiply by 0.4 to get your Fog Index, which roughly corresponds to the educational grade level at which your writing is aimed.

For example, in the letter in Figure 5–4, there are 111 words and three sentences in the first two paragraphs, for an average sentence length of 37 words:

$$111 \div 3 = 37$$

There are 23 "hard" words of three syllables and more (attention, introduction, consumer, personal, computer, reference, manual, inadver-

Figure 5—4. Sample letter for the Fog Index.

XYZ COMPUTER CO., INC.
18 Dos Road
Microchip Valley, CA 20134

Dear XYZ Personal Computer Customer:

It has been brought to our attention that in the introduction of our new consumer personal computer reference manual, an inadvertent error was made that resulted in misinformation about problem determination procedures in operation section 4-1 under "Checking Electrical Cables."

If the communications adapter cable referred to on this instructional page was included in the equipment purchased for the purpose of connecting with a modem, it should have a wrap plug which must be disconnected at the modem end before installation. Due to a computer programming error, the page referred to above offers a description contrary to this explanation and instructs the user to connect the wrap plug to the modem.

If you have already installed the communications adapter cable according to the original instructions, you may be having problems and your modem may not be operational. Problem determination procedures indicate that by disconnecting the wrap plug from the communications adapter cable the modem will be operational according to original specifications.

This oversight is regretted, but we are pleased to make a voluntary correction of this computer programming error. Your continued confidence in XYZ personal computers will be appreciated.

Sincerely,

F. Ormat Diskette
Vice President

tent, misinformation, determination, procedures, operation, electrical, communications, adapter, instructional, equipment, description, contrary, explanation, disconnected, installation) for a hard word index of 250:

$$23 \div 111 = 20$$

Adding the 37-word average sentence length to the 20 percent hard words, we get 57. Multiplying that by 0.4, we get a Fog Index of 22.8.

The clearest, user-friendly writing is in the range of 8 to 12—that is, between the eighth- and the twelfth-grade reading levels. At 22.8, the Fog Index of the sample letter means that readers would have to have more than ten years of college—at least a Ph.D.—to read the letter comfortably. That's way over the best grade levels for clarity.

Now apply the Fog Index to a sample of your own writing. If the Fog Index is too high, you'll have to use either shorter words or shorter sentences to bring it down.

Be Specific

Use solid, real-world words to give your writing a slice of life. Talk hot pink when you're talking color. Talk $10 off when you're talking discount. Talk pepperoni and melted mozzarella when you're talking pizza.

Be specific. Picture your idea for your readers in words that appeal to the five senses. That's the way to make them say, "I've got to have that now."

Words that give readers the experience of what you're "selling" are called concrete words. They're that solid. Concrete words are sensuous words: they refer to things you can see, smell, hear, taste, and touch.

If your idea is the greatest thing since canned beer, say so. The reader will get a better picture than if you just say that it's the greatest.

Concrete words are like triggers. They help readers recognize something they need. Or they turn what you're proposing into something they want. Like an array of pretty baubles on a counter, concrete words tempt readers, even the ones who are "just looking." Readers are impulse shoppers, too.

Dramatize Benefits: Sell Use

Words that offer a sample-in-print answer the reader's big question: What's in it for me?

Spell out the benefits of buying your idea in specific, concrete words. Dramatize. Sell *use* with words that give your reader the experience of "owning" your proposal. Don't say, *"Implementation of the optimum communications system will facilitate improved interface among all participants."* Say, *"We will all work better together if we can talk to each other quickly and easily."*

Put your ideas into action for the reader with words that bring them to life.

Choose Words with Sex Appeal

Words that trigger reactions are the kind that get a customer excited about what you're selling. They have "sex appeal."

Nouns and verbs—words that name persons, places, things, and actions—give writing energy. "Marilyn Monroe" is a noun, a name, and a few other things. "Beautiful" is an adjective. It doesn't have quite the same impact as the flesh-and-blood noun. Concrete nouns and active verbs anchor writing in the real world. Adjectives and adverbs describe, but they need nouns and verbs to keep them from floating away. For example, the reader would rather know that what you have in the pot is spinach than that it's green, leafy, sandy, and nutritious.

"Go for it" gets energy from an active verb. "It should be gone for" gets bogged down in the passive. Active verbs give writing excitement, and readers like to be where the action is.

But business has in the past favored the passive verb. It's true that you need it sometimes: *"Your credit rating was checked"* downplays the investigation better than *"We checked your credit rating."*

The passive can help you pass the buck: *"The file was lost"* removes the finger of blame pointed by *"I lost the file."* But in most cases your writing will be more vigorous if it makes clear who's doing what to whom.

Active verbs and concrete nouns give sentences sex appeal; passive verbs and abstract nouns don't.

Make It Imperative

Imperative verbs are useful in persuasion. In fact, sales talk seems to depend on the imperative: "Go for the gusto"; "Be all you can be"; "Have one built for you."

Imperative verbs build in action because they are already in the command form. They suggest, in a powerful way, what to do.

Sell "sizzle"

Words have denotation—direct, specific meanings, their dictionary meanings. And they have connotations, the extra meanings they collect through usage. These connotations are so powerful that psychologists can use word association to analyze your psyche.

In persuasion, you can use the connotations of words to advantage. They'll add "sizzle" to what you're selling. Seven-Up used to be just another soft drink until an ad campaign dubbed it the "Uncola," picking up all the connotations of no caffeine that its competitors couldn't match.

Because of their connotations, two of the best-selling words ever invented are "new" and "free." Add these to whatever you're promoting for a big boost in word power.

Names themselves are rich in connotations. Naming the new product, like naming the new baby, is an important decision. If you call the kid Percival after his grandfather, will you be setting him up to be called "sissy" at school? If the new soft drink, with real sugar and caffeine, is named "Jolt," will consumers get the message?

The more mileage you can get out of your words with their "ripple" effect, the more promise they'll have for the reader. The creative side of persuasion is finding ways to enrich the same old words with new meaning—with sizzle. And sizzle sells more steak.

Change the Context

Words can also pick up connotations from their surroundings. You can make them new and more motivating if you change their context. "Is your hair hungry?" asks an ad for Pantene shampoo. "This is no fare-y tale," says an ad promoting Delta's lower air fares.

A good way to gain acceptance for your new idea is to compare it with something the reader is already familiar with. Merrill Lynch, for example, used the slogan "A breed apart" to connect with the traditional bull-and-bear Wall Street image, yet pointed out the difference.

Puns, the commonest form of word play, put words in new contexts. Advertising copywriters like puns because they get attention and give some "play" to selling points. When Spam advertises, "A lot of meals. But not a lot of baloney," customers can enjoy the pun and perhaps think of Spam in a new way. So, Crane stationery takes "your words seriously," Kelly is out "to change America's tires," and Levelor window blinds proclaims, "Our love is blinds."

It's fun and it's creative to play with words. The more come-on your language has, the more appeal it will give to what you're selling. New language makes your idea or your product look new, too. But you have to control the "play." Being too clever with words can overshadow your message. The reader might admire your wit, but miss the point.

Words that work well in one context may backfire in another. Jokes and puns that seemed funny in person don't always get a laugh on paper. Use them with care; they can reach a reader when he's not in the mood—and boomerang.

Close the Gender Gap

More than half the readers out there are women, and you don't want to turn them off by using sexist language. English has had a built-in bias for years, but it's being corrected. Even Dr. Benjamin Spock changed the pronouns in his baby book when he realized that he'd been talking only about boy babies.

There has been some attempt to establish a new personal pronoun to bridge the gender gap. But "s/he" doesn't seem to be catching on. Instead of going for the wordy "his or her," change the whole passage to the plural and talk about "they." Or, alternate the "he's" and "she's" in the text. Or use "you."

Drop the feminine endings and just call her a poet or an author. "Poetess" and "authoress" sound condescending these days.

Use "representative" instead of "congressman." Use "mail carrier" and "police officer" in place of "mailman" or "policeman." And, of course, in phrases like "lady doctor" or "woman astronaut," the words "lady" and "woman" can be left out altogether.

Know your customer—and talk her language.

Be Natural

When you're talking your readers' language, you're already winning them over to your side. The best kind of advertising has always been word-of-mouth. So, write as you talk. You'll echo the reader, and it will put you both on more of a first-name basis. There's more chance you'll get a dialogue going. And you'll make your product sound familiar.

Good persuasive writing is also personal. It gets people into the act with words like "you" and "me," "I" and "we." It's no longer taboo to mention yourself in your writing. A good solid "I think" can help your credibility.

When people can see themselves in your writing, they're more likely to believe what you say. A natural, conversational style gives them the sense that you care about them, too.

In the medical profession, there's some concern about new doctors, who are said to learn more than 10,000 new words in medical school but don't know how to talk to their patients. Now, some schools are helping new graduates learn to explain medical procedures in language their patients will understand.

Don't Be Too Chatty

There's nothing more cloying, more off putting, than someone who wants to be too friendly on first acquaintance. In writing, don't be too chatty or too personal. Keep a discreet distance. You can be polite and still be friendly.

Be Positive

Psychologically, people are attracted to the positive. On the sales floor, a smiling, attentive salesperson can make you feel more like buying. Your readers will get more involved in your writing, too, if you're pleasant and positive. In fact, they'll pay more attention if your message begins with a positive statement.

People won't read on if you begin with the negative. The less you put the reader on the defensive, the more likely she'll be to get your message straight.

Your positive approach to your subject will create a positive attitude in the reader, too. Surrounded by yes, he'll feel more like saying yes himself. Meanwhile, he'll read. Readers like to associate with positive things.

And people behave in terms of their perceptions. Your positive, welcoming tone will make them feel at home. By reducing their sense of risk, you'll be motivating readers to take a chance.

Downplay the Negative

Never volunteer bad news. Recast it with a positive angle so that the reader will see it in the best light. For example, instead of saying, *"We are cancelling your subscription because you didn't pay your bill,"* preserve goodwill and future sales by collecting money this way: *"You can resubscribe by mailing your check today."*

Play up the positive. For pointers, see Figure 5–5.

Figure 5–5. Play up the positive.

No:	We can't ship the order until January 6.
Yes:	We'll ship your order promptly on January 6.
No:	I can't attend the meeting with you.
Yes:	I wish I could attend the meeting with you.
No:	We cannot pay the bill for six weeks.
Yes:	In six weeks, we will be able to pay the bill in full.
No:	You have failed to pay your bill.
Yes:	When you pay your bill, your credit rating will be improved.
No:	Thank you for letting us know about your bankruptcy proceedings and the foreclosure on your mortgage.
Yes:	Thank you for letting us know about your financial condition.
No:	We hope you won't forget to make this payment.
Yes:	We look forward to receiving your payment.
No:	If you decide to take our offer . . .
Yes:	When you decide to take our offer . . .
No:	You may wonder whether . . .
Yes:	We're sure you'll agree.
No:	You made an error in this letter.
Yes:	There is an error in this letter.

Be Honest

Being honest can win acceptance and sympathy. You can shore up a reader's trust by admitting to a weakness or a negative—if you follow it up with a strong point. Being straightforward at the right time helps credibility.

Never plant doubts. Suggest what to do, not what to avoid. Being positive gives your message stopping power. People will linger, and get the message. A friendly, positive approach creates the right atmosphere for persuasion.

The Message Is the Medium

Persuasive business writing makes readers an offer they can't refuse in words that meet the following criteria:

Get your readers' attention.
Echo their needs and wants.
Talk their language.
Dramatize the sizzle.
Create a positive selling situation.
Make reading easy.
Move your readers to action.

There's something special about persuasive language. It beckons with promise, flirts with poetry, and paints a picture for the reader. It's clear, brief, specific, natural, and positive.

Part Two
PERSUASION AT WORK

Chapter Six

Writing Persuasive Business Letters

Every business letter is basically a sales letter; the bottom line is a response. Whether you're asking for payment on a bill, trying to get an interview for a job, or simply requesting information, your underlying message is the same: Get back to me.

That's why persuasive strategies are ready made for business letters. Persuasion helps you get your reader involved enough in your words to want to do something about them.

Write Persuasive Letters

Letters are the most frequently used kind of writing in business. They are the written record of transactions, requests, and decisions. A letter is convenient and personal: it's delivered directly to your reader, who can read and refer to it, pass it on, and, of course, reply to it.

That is where persuasion will help, in assuring the reader's response. You have control of your message in letter writing, and can decide exactly what you want to say and how to say it. You can present the best case for your request and suggest to the reader how to respond. Persuasive strategies will give your letter the extra edge that makes the reader want to respond.

"I remain yours, as ever, blameless."

Drawing by Maslin; © 1984 The New Yorker Magazine, Inc.

Basics of Persuasive Letter Writing

Readers find it difficult to get interested in letters that seem to ignore them. However well you've explained your subject, they won't care very much about what you want unless you've considered their needs as well.

As we've seen, to get the response you want, you must first tap into the reader's self-interest. The odds are then in favor of her immediate involvement in what you say. Design every letter to acknowledge the reader's presence. Offer some kind of incentive for response. Answer the reader's basic question: What's in it for me?

1. Echo the reader.
2. Fit the message to the reader's needs.
3. Build the message on benefits.

A letter that brings good news or says yes to a request already offers benefits to the reader. Point them out to the reader. But all letters, whatever the message, can be built on benefits.

Collection letters, for example, should remind readers of the benefits of a good credit rating. Letters about employment should describe your talents as benefits for the prospective employer. And an adjustment letter, even when declining refunds or repairs, should offer a way to help solve the customer's problem.

Design the message to echo the reader. Fit the message to his needs, and build it on benefits. Everything about persuasive letter writing follows from these three basic rules.

Before You Write . . .

Persuasion in any medium, written or spoken, requires preparation. In order to echo the reader and build your letter on benefits, do your homework. Before you write, decide on strategy by using the three steps of Copythink:

1. Know your customer.
2. Know your product.
3. Find the Central Selling Point.

Running through the steps may take you just five minutes. Or it may take longer, depending on your knowledge of the reader, your access to information about him, and your understanding of what your message is. But you should allow time before you write to think these steps through, since they'll help you find the best way to present your message persuasively.

Know Your Customer

As Chapter One describes in detail, use the reader analysis checklist in Figure 1–1 to get a picture of your reader. Ask the six checklist questions: Who? What? When? Where? How? and Why? Jot down some answers. Try to imagine the reader reading your letter.

If you're writing a form letter that will go to many people, create a One-Customer Profile and write to that one person. Remember these points, common to all readers:

The reader is not, usually, waiting to receive your letter.
The reader has other things to do besides read it.
The reader won't be as involved with your written words as you are.

The results of your reader analysis will give you guidelines for custom-tailoring your message. Keep reminding yourself of the reader's presence as you write. After a while, your reader orientation will become automatic.

Know Your Product

Why are you writing this letter?

- *To settle a claim?* Then your letter will focus on how you propose to do it.
- *To ask for an interview?* Then the message will basically be about why the potential employer ought to interview you.
- *To ask for information about an order?* The message must be clear about when the order was placed and must focus on getting a date for delivery.

Get your message straight in your head first. It will be much clearer on paper. Jot down all the points you wish to make, number them in order of importance, and pick the One Big Idea.

Be sure that you have all the information you need before you write: the background on the claim, an updated résumé for the cover letter, the prior correspondence with your reader.

Find the Central Selling Point

Match what you want to what the reader wants. Present your One Big Idea in terms of a benefit for the reader.

For example, the main idea of a cover letter will be your qualifications for the job. Match those to benefits for the prospective employer. Say, *"My background in computer programming would mean you'd be hiring someone who needs no additional training."*

One Central Selling Point is the same for all business letters: goodwill. Even if your letter is just confirming an order or an appointment, you are still selling an image of your company. All business letters should convey goodwill, your interest in serving your readers and willingness to care about them.

The sense of your effort to be fair and understanding, even when you have to say no, builds priceless goodwill into every letter, and keeps customers coming back. Never be angry or abusive on paper. It spoils your image.

Plot Strategies for Every Letter

Persuasive tactics are also a matter of common sense. Here are points to remember for every business letter:

1. *Write to a name rather than to a company.* Get the right name, and spell it correctly. Use the reader's correct title, too. Make a quick telephone call to check name, title, and spellings.
   If it's impossible to get the name of your reader, you may use her title or think up an appropriate one: "Dear Editor," "Dear Human Resources Director."

2. *Use an appropriate salutation:* "Dear Mr. Smith"; "Gentlemen"; "Gentlemen and Ladies."
   If you don't know a woman's courtesy title, use her full name instead: "Dear Mary Jones."
   Don't use "Dear Sirs." It's outdated. And don't address a company run by women as "Gentlemen."

3. *In general, tell the reader what the letter is about as soon as possible—in the first sentence or the first paragraph.* Don't make her wade through the whole letter to find out why you're writing. The Good News format ensures that you won't make that mistake.

4. *Choose the Bad News format if you must give the reader disappointing news or say no.*

5. *Use the AIM format whenever you wish to add extra persuasion to your letters.*

6. *Talk the reader's language.* In general, use the conversational style in letters, to simulate a real conversation with the reader. She'll feel more at ease and more responsive to what you say.

7. *Be clear.* Be sure you've said what you thought you said.

8. *Be brief.* Keep letters to one page, about three or four paragraphs.

9. *Always call for action in the last paragraph.*

10. *Close with neutral phrases like "Sincerely," "Sincerely yours," or "Yours truly."* Don't sign off a letter with "Cordially" or get too chummy with "Warmest personal regards," or even "Best wishes," unless you do know the reader that well.

Select the Right Format

The three formats described in Chapter Three—the Good News format, the Bad News format, and the AIM format—are all you need to organize any business letter persuasively. Choose the one most appropriate to the purpose of your letter.

Because they're easy to remember, the formats save you the trouble of detailed outlining, and they'll come in especially handy when you're dictating.

The Good News Format

Use the Good News format to handle most business letters. It works persuasively even in the most routine letter because it lets the reader know immediately why you're writing.

Use it to say yes, to announce a meeting, to tell when an order was shipped or when credit was reinstated. The Good News format is always an option when you want to get the reader involved fast.

The Bad News Format

Saying no is more difficult than saying yes. The Bad News format will help you say no easily and convincingly. It's tailor made for collecting an overdue payment, for turning down a claim, for refusing requests, and for doing all these things persuasively.

The AIM Format

The AIM format is designed for selling. It will help you organize any message for maximum reader interest and motivation.

Always use the AIM format in sales letters. Use it, too, for letters about employment or fund-raising, or to give extra persuasion to a collection letter. Sell your ideas and your products with AIM. In any letter where you need a little salesmanship, the AIM format will provide the right psychological structure.

Know the Kinds of Business Letters

Almost any business letter you have to write will fall into one of two categories:

1. *Letters that ask*—for information, for approval, for an appointment, for an adjustment, for an order, for money.
2. *Letters that answer*—requests to which you must say yes or no.

Letters That Ask

Requests for information. Use the Good News format for requests for information. *Your objective:* A fast answer to your request.

Motivate the reader to respond as quickly as possible. Echo the reader. Offer a benefit for response. Suggest that you'll return the favor, perhaps by sending the reader a copy of the report for which he supplied information:

1. Put your request in the first paragraph:

   We'd like to order a copy of your report on "Corporations and the Two-Career Family" to help us plan on-site day-care centers in our company.

2. Explain exactly what you need in the second paragraph. Be clear and be specific:

   Over 50 percent of our employees have small children and we're interested in what your research has shown about absentee rates and company expenses when day care is provided.

3. Close, in the third paragraph, with a call to action, reminding the reader of your request and adding a sense of urgency. Suggest what you might do in return for his cooperation, and express your appreciation:

   Your study has been highly recommended to us and we look forward to receiving it in time to prepare a proposal due in October. And, of course, we'll let you know how the plan turns out.

Requests for adjustment. Use the Good News format. *Your objective:* Satisfaction, in the form of a reply or a solution.

Your tone is especially important in a claim letter. Don't get angry or abusive; it builds resistance in the reader. State clearly and objectively what is wrong and what you would like the reader to do about it.

Temper your complaint with at least one sentence that says something positive about the company or manufacturer, without obvious flattery: *"I've done business with your firm for ten years and have always been happy with the service I've gotten."*

1. Begin by stating your claim in an attention-getting way, connecting it with something familiar to the reader:

   Your new pasta maker has already given me quite a reputation for my spaghetti suppers. However, there was an attachment missing when I opened the box, and I'm writing to ask you to send it to me.

2. In the second paragraph, give full particulars of your claim:

   The missing part is the ravioli attachment, listed on the box as standard equipment. When I went back to Macy's to ask for it, the salesperson suggested I write directly to you. The model number of my pasta maker is 33-85-4, and the missing part number is

141. Since my warranty states that you cover all parts for 90 days
after purchase, I'm enclosing a copy of my sales slip showing that
I bought the machine just three weeks ago.

3. Close with a call to action and an expression of appreciation:

I'll appreciate your sending me the ravioli attachment as soon as
possible.

For extra persuasion, use the Bad News, or YES, format in a claim
letter:

1. Use the *you*-approach; connect with the reader in a positive way:

I've been a steady customer at Blossomdale's since 1980 because
I love your catalogue service.

2. *Explain:* Lead into the bad news or the complaint by giving
background and reasons for it:

When my recent order arrived so promptly, I was very happy. But
the dress was not the color I'd ordered, so I returned it, and was
told I'd still have to pay the postage charges.

3. *State* the bad news:

I certainly don't think it's fair to charge customers for postage and
insurance on orders that have been incorrectly filled, do you?

4. Close with a call to action, suggesting how to remedy the situation:

I'd appreciate it if you would credit my account for this $5.25
charge.

Requests for payment. Use the Bad News format. *Your objective:* To
collect the money owed and keep the customer.

Collection letters are usually designed in a series. The first letter is
just a friendly reminder. The second is firm, but offers to help the reader
in making the payment, perhaps by arranging a payment plan. The third
letter must show that you mean business; it sets a deadline for payment,
after which collection procedures or legal action will begin if payment is
not made.

Since it's much more expensive to take a customer to court than to
collect payment with a letter, it makes sense to design your collection
letters persuasively.

Your first collection letter in the series will prompt payment from
those who intended to pay but forgot, lost the bill, or have just been
procrastinating. Your second should pick up those who are habitually

slow about paying or who need some assistance in arranging payment. The third should motivate the real procrastinators. If it doesn't, your efforts must go toward collecting in a more forceful way; there *are* those who had no intention of paying in the first place.

The first letter about overdue payment should take the friendly-reminder approach, using the Bad News, or YES, format:

1. *You* connect with the reader in the first paragraph with a friendly, attention-getting opener, like one of the following, without ac-cusation:

   Have you forgotten something?

   Is something wrong?

   Perhaps there's a good reason why we haven't heard from you lately.

2. *Explain* by reminding the customer of the credit agreement. Ask if she has a question about the bill:

   We agreed when you opened your account to give you credit, and you agreed to pay your monthly bill within 30 days. If there is a question about your bill, please give me a call.

3. *State* the bad news. Mention the amount of money owed and when it was due. Combine this with benefits for paying:

   Your account is now more than 30 days overdue, but you can bring it up to date by putting your check for $92.80 in the mail today.

4. In your call to action, don't repeat the bad news. Be positive:

   With your account current, you won't want to miss our Spring Furniture Clearance, beginning next week with a private sale for charge customers only, in advance of announcement to the public.

If payment isn't made, in the second letter be firm:

[You]	We've been writing to you a lot lately about your account with us. By now, we had hoped to hear from you about it, too.
[Explain]	You've been a good customer, and we'd like to help you keep your account with us open. Prompt monthly payments maintain a good credit rating as well, a valuable asset these days.
[State]	But your bill is now more than 60 days overdue, and we will need a check for $92.80 by April 12 to keep your account open.

Call to action:	Send your check today in the enclosed addressed envelope to get prompt credit for your payment.

The third letter, if necessary, remains positive and objective, but clearly outlines procedure and deadlines. At this point, your approach should be quite straightforward:

[**You**]	We're sorry you've chosen to let your bill with us go unpaid so long.
[**Explain**]	Accounts that run 90 days behind schedule lose preferred status and get another status: scheduled for collection. Right now, that means you will have to pay your bill before you can use your charge account again.
[**State**]	Send your check for $92.80 today to restore charge privileges and prevent collection procedures scheduled to begin in 10 days.
Call to action:	We must receive your check by April 22 to stop further action.

Requests for contributions. Use the AIM format. *Your objective:* To obtain a contribution and make the reader feel good about making it.

The AIM format will help you present your cause as one the reader would like to be associated with, preferably as a sponsor.

1. Start with an attention-getting, reader-oriented first paragraph:

   [**Attention**] "I gave at the office."

2. Build interest in the next paragraph by talking benefits:

   [**Interest**] That makes a lot of sense when you can give to your favorite charity with one convenient paycheck deduction. This year, our United Fund drive offers you the choice of when and how much you'd like to give. Once you decide, you don't have to do another thing; your donation will be deducted automatically from your paycheck.

3. The third paragraph gives motivating details:

   [**Motivation**] For example, you can authorize a deduction of $5 over the next six pay periods that will provide a hot meal every day for two weeks to a shut-in. Or a one-time deduction of $15 that will make sure a preschooler has breakfast on weekday mornings for a month.

4. The call to action makes it easy:

> Check the box on the enclosed card that suits your sense of charity and return it to me. I'll see that your contribution gets where you want it to help most.

In fund-raising letters, a prominent postscript can give emphasis to an important, motivating point:

> P.S. Last year, our company had the highest rate of United Fund contributions in town. Let's do it again!

Requests for a job. Use the AIM format. Remember the first presentation of a cover letter in Chapter Three (Figure 3–6). *Your objective:* To get an interview.

Your echo of the reader and your promise of benefits are especially important in a cover letter. Search the advertisement or job description for clues to your audience. Echo the phrasing the employer has used to describe the position: *"I'm the kind of motivated, hard-working sales manager you're looking for."*

The benefits you'll promise are already on your résumé. You'll just have to interpret them in your cover letter as Central Selling Points, showing what your qualifications can do for the employer.

Doing your homework on the company will help you focus your message and will show you how to match your talents to the employer's needs. Find out about the company by reading its annual report, talking to people who've worked there, or checking on news articles that may have mentioned the firm.

Tone is important in this kind of letter. You don't want to sound pompous or conceited, but you do need to do some self-promotion. The proper tone can be achieved by turning your qualifications into benefits for the prospective employer:

1. Capture the reader's attention. The first paragraph of your cover letter should connect with something familiar to the reader and present you as a qualified applicant.

   One way to echo the reader is to mention how you heard about the opening or to use phrasing directly from the ad:

   > [**Attention**] The position you advertised in Sunday's *Times* sounds like just what I've been waiting for. I'm a seasoned, degreed, self-starter who'd like to work as a project analyst for Citicorp.

In this first paragraph, avoid clichés like "*I am writing to apply for.*" It's acceptable, but boring. A good attention-getter in the first paragraph is the name of a mutual acquaintance or of someone who already works at the company, if you're lucky enough to have a contact.

2. Next, build interest in your candidacy by using your Central Selling Point, translated as a benefit.

   [**Interest**] My five years as a financial control manager with Touche Ross and my M.B.A. from Harvard mean you'd be hiring a project analyst with demonstrated ability.

3. Motivate the reader by citing details from your résumé in the third paragraph. Be selective; you won't have room to mention everything:

   [**Motivation**] My experience includes price and cost analysis, long-range capital requirement projections, and high-visibility work with all levels of financial management. An article I wrote about developing financial models was published in the *Harvard Business Review* last spring.

4. Close with a call to action: ask for the interview:

   I'm ready for the challenge of a senior management position that will give me a chance to supervise a professional staff. At your convenience, I'd appreciate a chance to talk to you about a career with Citicorp.

Cover letters don't have to be long; one page is enough to make a persuasive case for your résumé. But they do have to accomplish one major task: connecting your experience and background to benefits for the employer, a Central Selling Point that is the key to a successful letter.

Letters That Answer

Replies to requests. Use the Good News format. *Your objective:* Goodwill.

Replies to letters of inquiry should be brief and direct. Sometimes they can be handled in one paragraph:

   We're shipping your order today, and you should have it by Monday. Thanks for ordering from XYZ Corporation.

When you can answer yes, your letter of reply is an easy one to write. Use the Good News format to say yes right away.

Saying no takes more thought, to preserve goodwill and keep the customer. The Bad News, or YES, format will help you deliver the message:

[You]	We're always delighted to hear from viewers about programs they've enjoyed on Channel 14.
[Explain]	And we've certainly had plenty of requests for the transcript of Tuesday night's show on the new tax laws. We wish we could send it right out to everyone who has asked.
[State]	The trouble is that the transcript won't be available for two more months because of a copyright problem.
Call to action:	If you don't mind waiting, we'll be happy to keep your name on our list, and will send you the transcript you've requested as soon as it's ready.

Replies to claim letters. Use the Bad News format to say no. *Your objective:* To keep the customer and maintain goodwill.

Start such letters with an expression of understanding or an echo of the reader's situation:

[You]	We can understand how you felt when your carpet wasn't installed in time for your party Saturday night.
[Explain]	The order slip for installation was put through the day you came in, and delivery was scheduled by our dispatchers for last Tuesday.
[State]	As I mentioned when I called you, a truck strike stopped all our deliveries this week, and as a result, much to our regret, we were unable to get your carpet there for installation.
Call to action:	To make up for the delay, we'd like to offer you a 10 percent discount on installation. Your carpet is at the top of our schedule; please give me a call to let me know when you'd like us to bring it over.

Even—especially—in the Bad News letter, you can add a touch of sales talk, perhaps in an attention-getting postscript:

P.S. You might like to include our new Protecto-pads® in your order. They're great for heavy-duty areas, and on sale now at 25 percent off.

If you can say yes to a claim, follow the Good News format:

> Your ravioli attachment for your new PastaFasta® is on its way, in plenty of time, we hope, for your next dinner party.
>
> Thanks for letting us know about the missing part. It's a big help to hear from customers when things aren't quite as expected.
>
> We're glad to know you like the PastaFasta®, too. As a gourmet cook, you might also be interested in our new Cutsalotta® kitchen helper. Take a look at the enclosed brochure and let us know if you'd like to order one.

A yes letter is a good place to talk future sales; the customer's already in a positive frame of mind.

Replies to requests for credit. Use the Bad News format when you have to say no. *Your objective:* To keep the customer.

Even when you can't make good on a request for credit, your letter should create a good image of your company and offer an incentive to keep the customer coming back.

Sometimes you don't have to refuse outright. You can simply say, *"All our business is on a cash basis right now."*

[You]	We're looking forward to having you as a customer at Blossomdale's and thank you for your application for credit.
[Explain]	Charge privileges help you buy at your convenience, with the option of paying on a monthly basis. We try to give every customer who has established a good credit rating the privilege of an account.
[State]	Your application has been carefully considered, and we hope to welcome you as a charge customer when you've acquired a credit rating. Your bank can best advise you on the way to do this.
Call to action:	Meanwhile, you might want to look into our temporary charge card service so that you won't miss out on any of this fall's exciting sales. Stop in at our Customer Service office and ask for Ms. Clark. She'll be happy to arrange it for you.

Write Motivating Form Letters

Many of the business letter situations described in this chapter can be handled with a form letter designed to reach a number of customers.

These can follow the same formats as individualized letters and be just as persuasive if you've targeted your audience well.

Analyze the range of readers your letter will go to and design a One-Customer Profile. For example, in writing a series of collection form letters, you might divide readers into good-risk, poor-risk, and procrastinator categories.

Form letters have a public relations problem because they lack the personal touch and give away the fact that the same letter is going to many different people. Computers have solved this problem to some extent; now you can print the reader's name and address in the same type font as your letter, for an individualized touch.

You should never send a form letter when you're looking for a job. And prepackaged, impersonal replies to claims are never very persuasive.

The form letter (Figure 6–1, see p. 88) works because it is well focused on the reader's interests. A modified Bad News format is used to spark interest in paying a bill. Persuasive AIM also plays a part in motivating the customer.

Package What You Write

First impressions, in letters as well as in personal appearance, do count. The visual appeal of your letter is an important factor in its persuasiveness. Here are three guidelines for giving your letters an attractive visual appearance:

1. *Make it look easy to read:*
   - Use lots of white space, at least one inch of margin on all four sides.
   - Keep letters short.
   - Paragraph frequently.

2. *Make it letter-perfect:*
   - Proofread for spelling and grammatical errors.
   - Insist on typo-free letters; one mistake can make enough "noise" to drown out your message.

3. *For faster reading, emphasize important points:*
   - Use underlining.
   - Use lists like this.
   - Paragraph frequently to highlight separate ideas.

Figure 6–1.   Harvard Business Review letter.

In Business, it's give and take.

We've sent you the first issue of Harvard Business Review and
your complimentary booklet which we offered when you subscribed.
Now you're really in Business.

So it's time to remind you that our second invoice is enclosed.
We realize it probably seems insignificant beside the more pressing
bills that loom large every business day.

Yet for the small amount of that invoice, the finest minds in the
business world are writing to executives and professionals like
you -- to inform, guide, challenge. It would be a shame if a little
forgetfulness deprived you of their insights.

Unless there is something seriously wrong (or you have already
mailed your payment), please return the invoice together with your
check in the self-addressed envelope.

Take care of Business by sending us your payment today.

Cordially,

Ralph B. Titus
Circulation Director

RBT/hbb

Reprinted by permission of Harvard Business Review.

Chapter Seven

Writing Persuasive Memos

The memo is tailor made for persuasion. Short, time-saving, and informal, it's already familiar to your readers as an accepted kind of in-house writing. Because you'll know many of these readers personally and can talk their language, with a memo you can motivate response more easily. As a written message that can move through all levels of the company, the memo also lends itself to whatever maneuvers the politics of office life may require.

The Politics of Persuasion

With a memo, you can achieve a number of objectives. You can, for example:

- Influence a much wider audience than you might by telephone or at a meeting.
- Introduce yourself to those higher up in the organization.
- Keep the lines of communication open with people you'd rather not deal with face to face.
- Save time by asking for a memo from someone who is demanding of your attention.
- Keep track of what people said they'd do and motivate them to do it.

*"Loved your last memo, Ted. You're beginning
to find your own voice."*

Drawing by Lorenz; © 1984 The New Yorker Magazine, Inc.

- Clarify instructions, announce decisions, explain procedures in a well-organized way.
- Protect your own performance by keeping a memo record of it.

There may be disadvantages to writing it down, of course. If one of the purposes of putting it in writing is to keep a record, you should do so with discretion. For example, very personal remarks, humor, or private jokes won't be appropriate in the company files where most memos end up. And people who write too many memos are just adding to the general overload of paperwork in most offices. A quick conversation in the hall may be more persuasive. And a telephone call can be faster.

Yet a memo designed to "sell" its facts and ideas is an extremely effective tool for motivating others and for supporting your own career effort. In writing, you're in charge of the message and can design it more carefully to motivate the response you want. Your reader may feel more obliged to respond to a memo than to a telephone call; in addition, she can keep the memo as a reminder and refer to it. For example, your short memo welcoming a supervisor back from a business trip or vacation may still be on her desk a week later to remind her of your goodwill.

Some people have become famous—or infamous—for their memos. David O. Selznick's at MGM were memorable enough to be published. Henry Kissinger's well-timed summaries of political situations were said to be very influential in shaping national policy during one administration; Alexander Haig's case of "memo-itis" was notable mainly for its irritation value. And memos Supreme Court Justice William H. Rehnquist had written were considered crucial evidence in the hearings to appoint him chief justice.

A reputation for clear, succinct memos can do a great deal for your career. You'll be known to some members of your organization only by what you write. In the files, your writing should go on speaking well of you. As the Latin word *memorandum* indicates, memos are "to be remembered." It's worth knowing how to write them well.

Memo Strategy

A clear memo that gets to the point in the first paragraph is persuasive in itself. And although memos can run to several pages or more, a short, one-page memo is one of the most effective tools of persuasion. Because it's short, it's bound to get read, not stalled in a pile on someone's desk to be read later. And if you keep your memos clear and concise, people will begin to recognize and respect you as a person who can get things done.

But memos are often written in a hurry and under pressure, dashed off on the spur of the moment to take care of immediate business. And although there may be no getting around a time crunch, a few minutes spent running through the basic Copythink steps will give your memos a strategic edge even when you do have to send them off in a hurry.

Know Your Customer

Audience analysis for the memo is usually quite simple. You already know most of your readers through day-to-day contact and have some firsthand knowledge of their interests. Even so, you should always run through your who-what-when-where-how-and-why routine just to switch your focus to the all-important reader's point of view. A shortcut method for the memo: Simply ask "Who?" and "What?" to give you a miniprofile on your reader and what he or she needs to know.

Memos frequently have more than one reader, however. Although they are usually sent just to the person who must take action on them, you may wish to send copies to others for their information and should keep their concerns in mind, too, as you write. Use the One-Customer Profile to make it easy to address this peripheral audience, especially to ensure that you offer them enough background to understand the memo.

A good way to reach a diversified audience on a long distribution list is to tailor just your first paragraph differently for each group. For example, suppose that your report on a recent business trip will go not only to your immediate superior but to the accounting, marketing, and legal departments as well. Design different opening paragraphs highlighting an aspect of the trip that will appeal to each group's special interests. Then, just add on the same follow-up details for each. You'll generate interest from all readers this way, and allow them to choose how much of your memo they must read.

Know Your Product

The best way to keep your memos short and to the point is to know what you want to say before you write. Ask yourself, What is my message here? Write down the points you wish to make, in any order. Just get what's in your head down on paper.

Now, quickly number the points in order of importance. What's the *big* idea here?

Stick to One Big Idea

Memos can tend to be catchall messages for whatever's on the writer's mind at the moment. Don't let that happen to yours. Focus them. Pick a major point and stick to it. Perhaps some of your other points can be related to it; if not, they belong in a different memo.

Simply by taking a few moments to find the One Big Idea, you'll do wonders for everything you write, and especially for your memos. Readers remember and understand a message better when it's focused for them. If it isn't, they'll pick out their own focus, perhaps entirely different from what you intended. And that's not a very good persuasive strategy.

Select the Right Format

If the purpose of the memo is to speed things up and keep the flow of information moving within the company, the most important element in that momentum is a structure that can be read quickly.

Once you've decided what your memo is about, pick an appropriate structure for it from the three persuasive letter formats in Chapter Four. These formats translate readily for use in the memo. They're easy to remember; and with practice, you'll find organizing your memos quite simple, even when you dictate them.

The basic memo design is abbreviated for speed, using time-saving headings that direct the message, alert the reader to its subject, and make the memo easy to refer to. In the memo, unlike the letter, there's no "Dear Mr. Jones" opening or "Sincerely yours" ending. Simple headings take care of addressing the reader. And when you've finished what you have to say, just stop.

The basic format is so standardized that many companies use pre-printed forms. Don't try to innovate here; the established format lowers reader resistance by meeting expectations and giving your message a level of acceptance at first glance. Yet, within this format, you can make your mark with clear, brief, and well-organized writing.

Use every visual method you can to make your memos look easy to read and to save time for busy readers. Right from the beginning, take advantage of the memo's headings to focus your message:

TO:	Fill in the name and title of the person who must act on this memo. Send copies for the information of others. If the memo will go to several readers, alphabetize their names or list them according to rank.
FROM:	Your name and title, initialed by you.
DATE:	The dateline often appears alone at the upper right instead of with the other headings.
SUBJECT:	Give your memo a good title. Like a newspaper headline, it should highlight your main idea for the reader. Say *"How the Bank Can Attract Customers Under the New Tax Law"* instead of just *"The New Tax Law"* for example. Don't refer to your subject line in the body of your memo; it's annoying to read, *"In regard to the above-mentioned subject,"* and a waste of words.

The memo format should look like this:

April 2, 1987

TO: John Smith, Vice President

FROM: Mary Alden, Marketing Manager

SUBJECT: Marketing Department Summer Vacation Schedule

As you requested, I've coordinated the vacation dates for my department with our marketing calendar so that there won't be any slowdown during our busiest weeks in August when we're launching the campaign.

Tim Jones and Alison Foster will be taking the first two weeks in June; Bob Matthews, Jim Crain, and John Bartlett are scheduled for the second two weeks; and Susan Maxwell will take the first week in July. I'm planning to be away July 8–15.

This way, at least one person who is working on the campaign will be in the office at all times, and everybody will be there from July 16 on.

Let the structure of your memo show.

- Use headings to divide sections of the memo, even a short one. They'll indicate your major points to the reader and save time for you by eliminating the need for transitions.
- Take advantage of underlining to emphasize important words or topics.
- Use short paragraphs to make reading easy.
- And think about numbering or listing each of your points for handy reference when it's appropriate. For example:

  1. The new company shuttle bus will operate from 5 P.M. to 7 P.M. to take employees to the station after work.
  2. On Fridays, the shuttle will begin at 4 P.M.
  3. There will be no charge for this service.

The Good News format. The best way to organize a memo is to use the Good News format. It allows you to get to your main point first, and as we've seen, that's always the most persuasive thing you can do in the memo.

At the beginning of any piece of writing, you'll always have the reader's undivided attention for at least a few seconds. The Good News format helps you use that time to advantage. Since most people will read at least the first sentence or paragraph of a message, your fast-start opening satisfies their curiosity about your subject, increases their involvement with your message, and helps them understand it better.

Because it's organized in an inverted pyramid like a news story, the Good News format also gives readers the option of choosing how much they'll read. And it helps you keep the memo short. For example:

Since the new tax law cuts out interest deductions on the consumer loans that have been our steadiest business, we've got to offer something better to attract customers. In my opinion, we ought to put all our efforts behind the bank's new home equity program.

The second paragraph will then explain details:

As you know, interest on second mortgages is still deductible, so customers can borrow on their homes to make major purchases they used to finance through our consumer loans. I think we can offer an interest rate on home equity that will beat the competition, and make it fast and easy to get a loan without the usual red tape.

Always end with a call to action:

I'd like to go over this with you in detail before next week's meeting with the president. Wednesday at 3, in my office?

The Good News format, with its fast-start opening, will give even the most routine memo a persuasive edge. Readers will understand better and act faster when they have an overview of the entire message first.

Use the Good News format to present recommendations, to answer requests with an up-front yes, to summarize results of a meeting or a business trip, even to write a note of thanks or congratulations. Following your summary opening, you can present the rest of the details in whatever way you wish, chronologically, in descending order of importance, or by numbered points.

The Bad News format. Memos can, of course, also contain disappointing or bad news. When you recognize that your reader may not welcome what you have to say in your memo or may disagree with you, the Bad News format offers you a better psychological structure for your message.

You don't want to put the reader on the defensive in the first paragraph by announcing the worst. Instead, build up to the bad news and prepare the reader.

Start off with a neutral, you-oriented statement:

Your request for more time on the Taylor project arrived on my desk this morning.

Then offer an explanation for the bad news to come:

> As you know, we're running behind schedule in setting this up, and
> since the board meets next week to consider our recommendations,
> we'll need to get the proposal in final form by this Friday.

Now give the bad news:

> I wish we could extend the deadline, too. But maybe you and I can
> go over your draft and finish it together on time.

Add the call to action:

> Give me a call first thing in the morning so that we can arrange a
> time tomorrow to get to work on this.

Remember, never repeat the bad news. Use the last paragraph as a call
to action.

The AIM format. You won't need hard-sell language to be persuasive in the memo; in fact, the language of the memo generally should be
fairly low-key and informal. Instead, use the AIM format to organize
your message in a motivating way. This format is especially useful for
proposing new ideas, for motivating the performance of other people,
for handling customer complaints and adjustments, and, of course, for
actual selling.

An attention-getting first paragraph is essential in getting through
to a busy reader:

A *stands for attention.* Use one of the grabbers (see Chapter Three
for suggestions). A good one for the memo is a short question that can
be answered yes:

> Wouldn't you rather leave work early than take extra time for
> lunch?

Getting to the point in the first paragraph is always attention-getting,
too. And your firsthand knowledge of most of your potential readers
should help you devise good openers that will get their attention.

I *stands for interest.* Build on benefits: match what you want to what
your reader needs or wants for a Central Selling Point that increases
involvement:

If we closed at 4:30 P.M. instead of 5, we could all beat the rush hour after work. And have extra time at the end of the day at home. Shortening the lunch hour to allow for this would mean we'd all be back at our desks by 1, with a shorter afternoon ahead.

M *stands for motivation.* Add facts here to back up your selling point. Use testimonials or statistics to provide evidence:

Companies who've tried these new hours say that there has been a noticeable increase in productivity. Boswell reports that since the new schedule went into effect six months ago, there is less absenteeism among its employees.

The call to action. Always end with a suggested next step, a built-in response that helps the reader move in your direction:

To make this a companywide decision, we'd like to hear from you about this proposed new schedule. Just drop the enclosed card with your vote and comments in the box as you come through the lobby.

The structure of your memo is the key to its success as an action-getting message. Short, clear, to-the-point, the memo can work for you as a prime motivator for getting work done.

Find the Central Selling Point

The Central Selling Point matches the most important feature of your product, your message, with a benefit for the reader. The benefits you offer are crucial to persuasion.

Even the most routine memo can have a selling point: it offers an effortless, fast read. This should be one benefit you offer in everything you write. Whether you're actually selling something or not, the speed and clarity of your memos reward the reader for reading and allow him to get on with things, rather than have to puzzle out what you meant. Match what you want—to get your memo read—with what the reader wants—to read it fast and get done.

To find a Central Selling Point for promoting an idea, a directive, or a procedure, pick out the unique or most important feature of your message. Let's say that you have to write a memo to all employees asking them to stop calling Dial-A-Joke during business hours. It's running up the telephone bill, to say nothing of what you imagine is a great deal of

downtime on the telephone. The thrust of your message is something like
"Cut it out!" but you can't put it that way.

What's in it for employees to follow your directive? What benefit
can you offer that will motivate compliance? You'd like to maintain the
office policy of allowing personal use of the telephones, giving employees
a sense of freedom and responsibility that they seem to appreciate.

Sell use. Remind them of the telephone privilege and that you'd like
to continue to make it available. That's the benefit they'll get for doing
as you request, a Central Selling Point that will be much more persuasive
than a mere threat to end all personal calls. Here's an example using the
Bad News format and a you-approach:

> We all could use a laugh now and then.
>
> Sometimes the pressure gets to you, and you lose your sense of hu-
> mor. A telephone call to Dial-A-Joke seems to offer a little relief.
>
> But are things around the office so pressured that we need to make
> calls to Dial-A-Joke at the rate of nearly a hundred a week, just to
> get a laugh?! At 25 cents a call, you can imagine how this is adding
> up on our telephone bill every month.
>
> Something everybody seems to enjoy about working here is the per-
> sonal use of the telephone, to call home, to check on the kids, to
> make an appointment. If we want to keep this privilege, the Dial-A-
> Joke calls will have to go.
>
> No joke!

A Central Selling Point gives your reader motivation to respond to
and act on what you say. Build your message on benefits. Sell use. And
always strive to make your memos fast and easy to read—that's a benefit
for every reader.

Adopt a Conversational Style

A memo is the next best thing to a telephone call in terms of immediacy,
and it should sound as friendly and informal as you do in person. Try to
write as you talk.

The conversational style, which reaches all readers in a familiar-
sounding language, will give your memos a personal tone that's persuasive in itself. Use contractions, personal pronouns, short words, and

short sentences to reproduce the sound of your voice. And, on occasion, a hand-written memo can be very effective when you want a really personal touch.

A fancy memo style, as impressive as you may think it is, only slows communication and gives the reader too much room for misunderstanding what you say:

> It is of the first order of business that the stock option plan be implemented for presentation to the board of directors by the second week in September.

Is "the second week in September" the deadline for completing the plan or for presenting it to the board? It's not very clear. Better to use simpler language and a more natural tone:

> We have to complete the stock option plan by the second week in September so that we can present it to the board of directors.

Another common but ineffective memo style is one that sounds like a telegram:

> Yours of the 25th received. Send all receipts to the order department. Plans made for meeting with J. B. on return.

This is certainly short, but it isn't very clear. The memo sounds businesslike just because the sentences are so clipped, but it's hard to understand. You're not writing a telegram; use full sentences, and avoid jargon.

Develop a style for your memos that readers can understand quickly. The style you use when you talk is already geared for fast delivery and understanding; try to reproduce that on paper. It's probably better, however, to avoid getting too slangy or informal. There's a happy medium somewhere between the college alumni newsletter style and the too pretentious. For example, this style is *too* informal:

> Well, old Biff has done it again. Wow! Vice president at 30! This is one for the books, folks, and you'll just have to ask him yourself how he managed to pull it off—atta boy there, Biff!!!

But this is too formal:

> It has come to my attention that Mr. J. Biffington Furbes has been promoted to the position of vice president here at Dagwood Tool Company.

A happier medium:

> We're pleased to announce that Biff Furbes has just been promoted.
> He'll be the new vice president of sales at Dagwood Tool.

Talk Yes

Remember to be positive; say *I wish we could extend the deadline*,
instead of *We can't extend the deadline.* Say *You can expect your order
the first week in May,* not *You can't expect your order until the first week
in May.* A positive approach is always more persuasive because readers
accept good news better than bad.

Paint the Picture

Use active verbs: say *I sent you the order last week,* rather than *The
order was sent to you last week.* And try for the reality of concrete nouns
rather than the ponderous abstract. For example, which of the following
messages would readers understand faster?

> Management is cognizant that employees are availing themselves
> of office copiers to reproduce documents of a personal nature. It is
> hereby requested that any such activity not pertaining to company
> business be terminated.

Or:

> Please don't use the copying machines for anything but Dagwood
> Tool business.

Give the Memo Momentum

Any time you slow a reader down with a writing style that's full of ab-
stractions and hard-to-understand words, you're slowing down his response; the action you want is delayed while he spends time just figuring
out what you mean. A clear, familiar writing style that uses short words
and short sentences removes that barrier and enhances whatever persuasive strategy you use.

The most persuasive memos have three basic ingredients: speed,
clarity, and the reader's immediate understanding of your message:

- Keep your memos brief, so that they'll get read.
- Make them clear, using familiar language and a strong structure so that there can be no misunderstanding.
- Start fast, so that the reader gets your main point first.
- When you've finished what you have to say, just stop.

Chapter Eight

Putting Some Sell into Your Reports

Writing a report can be a chore. You have to research your subject; get all the data together; sit down and try to make sense of it; organize your findings; and, finally, write them up so that somebody else can understand them. Somewhere in the process you'll inevitably hit a snag that holds you up for days; or, just because it looks like a big job, you'll put off starting the report until you're almost at the deadline.

But writing reports doesn't have to be so laborious and unpleasant a task. What you've already learned about putting persuasion into your letters and memos works equally well in longer pieces of writing like reports, and, in fact, will help you make short work of them.

What Is a Report?

A business report is a written document that presents information—facts and ideas—to other people for their decision and action. As such, it should be convincing and credible. Its data and organization should be designed for quick reading and understanding. And it has to be clear to an often large and diverse audience of business readers.

Business reports should be written in an objective—but not impersonal—style, a shade more formal, perhaps, than the style you're used to using in letters and memos, in order to support a sense of your accurate and fair approach. A report is usually "packaged" in a standard order, either one your company prefers or the well-accepted structure presented in this chapter.

Business reports are based on research, the same kind you used to do for papers in college or high school. But the business report has a far more extended life than does the average term paper. Once the term paper is written and graded, it has fulfilled its purpose. A finished report, however, moves on to become the basis for further activity, such as:

Making decisions
Informing people at various levels of the company
Solving problems
Assessing business propositions
Acting on information

The function of business reports, like that of letters and memos, is to make things happen. And the techniques of persuasion will energize yours with the necessary reader motivation to do so.

Unfortunately, too many reports are still being written as if they were term papers, full of research that hasn't been sorted out for functional use, organized as if readers had the leisure to plow through pages of material before getting to the main point, and written in the ponderous, formal prose that causes a reader's eyes to glaze over by the end of the first page. Frequently, nothing happens because of these reports; either the reader loses interest or is held up trying to figure out what the report means—and, however mildly, resenting the wasted time.

Build In Persuasion

The ten rules of persuasive business writing and the three steps of Copythink offer you a simple method for writing reports that will keep readers interested and get results. Although what follows will explain many of the details and techniques involved in report writing, this chapter isn't intended as a complete guide to report writing. Instead, it will show you ways to improve on your present methods and to put the motivating factor of persuasion into what you write.

The three most persuasive techniques you can use in a report are, for example:

1. *Give your conclusions and recommendations first.* This satisfies your readers' need to know what you found out and gives them the option of stopping here or reading the rest of the report.

2. *Use planned repetition—summary, restatement, expanded detail—throughout the report.* This lets readers choose what and how much to read without missing your main ideas.
3. *Make the organization of the report crystal clear with visual emphases like headings, underlining, lists, and a good table of contents.* These, too, will offer your readers the option of easily choosing what they do and don't have to read.

If these three recommendations surprise you, it's only because you may be used to reading reports organized in the old-fashioned chronological way, where you have to read the whole report from beginning to end. Nobody has time for that any more. As much as you'd like them to savor your well-turned phrases, readers are busy and forced to skim. Accept that important fact about the contemporary reader and design your report to echo the reader's need for fast information.

For persuasion, you must think of your report in two stages of organization, one for writing and one for reading. The first stage is the actual order in which you write the report, from your own analysis of data to your conclusions.

The second stage is the order for reading. This will be just the reverse of the way you wrote the report: your conclusions will come first and your supporting data second. Once you've completed the writing of the report from natural beginning to end, you must reorder it for your readers' immediate comprehension and use, to avoid making them wade through the whole report to find out your conclusions.

As in all persuasion, you must allow your "customers" to feel that they can make up their own minds. If your report is organized properly, they can decide for themselves how much they need to read. And in an information age, particularly in communicating with reports, you must be able to transmit what you know in a form that follows its function: fast, readable information, ready to be used by the people who have to act on it.

Persuasive techniques will help you achieve any—or all—these objectives:

• Make sure that your report gets read and accepted, by organizing it to echo your readers' needs and interests.
• Build understanding of complicated issues with a large audience.
• Convince your readers that what you say is trustworthy and worth their consideration.
• Sell your recommendations and proposals.
• Gain the support of your superiors.

Plan a Persuasive Report

Reports, which can range from a one-page proposal to a book-length study, require more planning than most other kinds of business writing, and not only because they tend to be longer. As a primary method of communicating important and complex information to diverse groups of readers at the same time, reports need to be carefully designed.

Take a look at your own company's annual report, for example. It's put together primarily for the stockholders, to give them a yearly overview of their investment. But an annual report also goes to accountants, lawyers, and government agencies, and is used as a public relations tool to promote the company image. The audience for annual reports is a big one, with competing interests.

Yet most annual reports meet this communication challenge well, by arranging information in clear categories, using lots of graphics and pictures, and offering detailed financial sheets as support. The report gives a snapshot view of the company, clear and easy for most readers to understand at a glance. Admittedly, annual reports aren't as objective and detailed as you might wish, yet that is a deliberate persuasive strategy aimed to present the company at its best and to win over a large audience.

Your own reports may not need to reach so many readers. But they'll require the same deliberate planning and strategic organization to win acceptance of your findings and motivate response. The prewriting steps are, perhaps, the most important. You'll need to plan your research as well as your writing; you'll need to know or to decide on the basic purpose of the report and how much it will cover. And you'll have to know how to "package" the report in an accepted and functional way for your audience.

By using the steps of Copythink, you can do the prewriting homework on audience, purpose, and motivation that will set the stage for researching and writing a persuasive report.

Know Your Customer

The first question you should ask in setting up a report strategy is the sixth one on your reader analysis checklist: "Why?" Even before you begin to analyze your audience or organize a strategy for a business report, you need to have a clear idea of why you are writing it.

The purpose of all business reports is to generate action. Sometimes that action is simply understanding, and the purpose of the report is just to gather information in an organized way. Most reports, however, are analytic; that is, they not only present information, but analyze it for the reader's use.

If your boss asks you to write a report about absenteeism, get him to define that further. What absenteeism is he talking about anyway? Is it a problem throughout the company, or just with office or plant workers, or on one shift? Does he want you to offer recommendations on how to reduce absences or simply to find out what's causing them?

Once you've defined the problem, write down a simple and specific statement of purpose and keep it in front of you as you plan the report. For example, your purpose statement might be, *"To find causes of absenteeism on the first shift in the Hartford plant and recommend ways to reduce it."*

The other "why" of question 6 is "Why should the reader respond?" One answer will serve for all report readers: because the report is organized to fit the readers' need for fast information and shows clearly what action to take. This answer determines the way you arrange the report for your readers, with your findings up front.

Who Will Read This Report?

The primary audience for your report is probably going to be the person who assigned or requested it. But don't assume in writing a report that yours is an audience of one. In fact, most reports have a much wider audience than just your immediate superior or associates, circulating to various parts of the company—and sometimes externally as well—to inform and gain support for business decisions.

Start from the basic premise of business audience analysis: all the possible readers for your report are most interested in how it will affect their own jobs and power base.

Now, identify what we'll call your first-level readers, those who requested the report or who have a big stake in its results. Ask yourself who cares the most about the problem or situation that your report covers, who will act on your findings, and who will want to take credit for solving the problem.

Next, think about the implications of your report for people in other divisions of the company. These will be what we'll call your second-level, or peripheral, readers. Reports usually move upward in an organization, to higher authorities. Remember that as your report moves up or down the company chain of command, your readers will have very different concerns; people at the top will be more interested in the company image and its productivity than will readers at a lower level who may do the work.

If, for example, you make recommendations, who will have to carry them out? If you propose a budget, who will have to approve it or operate within it? If yours is a technical report, will it go to people who won't be familiar with the situation or the terminology used to describe it?

Make a list of all the potential first- and second-level readers these questions reveal. You'll know some of them personally and can supply additional details about their attitudes and professional background. For those you don't know from firsthand acquaintance, knowledge of their job titles and responsibilities will help you understand some of their main concerns.

Construct a One-Customer Profile for your report by choosing common characteristics from among the various groups of readers you've identified. For example, even though your report might be going to groups as disparate as engineers, lawyers, and marketing specialists, you can still find areas of common concern that your report must reflect: aim it, for example, at the people in those groups who must act on your findings, those with decision-making power. For everyone else, the report will be mainly informational, but they'll appreciate being regarded as part of management. You can provide special sections of your report for those who need more background information.

Remember, to persuade, you must always echo your readers and fit your message to their needs.

What Does the Reader Need to Know?

The extent of your readers' knowledge will determine how much research you'll have to do for the report.

Some of your readers will be very familiar with the subject of your report and won't need much additional information or case history to understand what you say. If these are your first-level readers, your research job will be fairly easy. However, in the second level of readers there may be many who have very little knowledge of your subject and who will need a more complete explanation of the problems you address.

You can manage to write for both groups of readers without boring one or ignoring the needs of the other; background information can be included at the beginning of your report. Your readers themselves can then decide if they need to read it.

In doing your reader analysis, you should also ask what your reader will have to do because of the report: act, decide, pass it on, just read it.

When and Where Will the Reader Read It?

Because they're usually longer than one page, reports don't always get the immediate attention you'd hope your hard work would demand.

But if you've designed the report for the fast read and the busy reader, it will be instantly appealing for the seeming lack of effort required to understand it.

In itself, that will keep your report off the "read-later" pile on people's desks. Remember that reports sent within the company are going to appear at a desk, during the press of business, and perhaps under a deadline, along with all the other paperwork that has to be read somehow.

A "read-later" pile sometimes goes home for the weekend, and there your reader may have more leisure to peruse what you've said. But you should plan your report for on-the-job reading, and make it look effort-less enough to get read then and there.

How Will the Report Affect the Reader?

It's vital in analyzing your readers to think about how what you say will be received by them. For some, your report may have a neutral effect. But most readers will react, agreeing or disagreeing with your findings. That reaction is within your control.

Depending upon your readers' involvement with the problem you're discussing, you'll have to gauge the emotional impact of your report in terms of how what you say will affect their jobs. Some readers may be upset if it recommends changes in their responsibilities or routines. If you have bad news, you already know that you'll have to present it persuasively.

You can dilute the effect of disappointing or bad news by the way you organize the information in your report. But you'll need to know first what your readers' attitudes and possible reactions may be.

As in all persuasive writing, the most important step you can take is to consider your report from your reader's point of view. You cannot persuade anybody until you connect with what's already in that person's head. That, as you already know, is the basis of persuasive strategy.

Use the questions from the reader analysis checklist to help you figure out what's going on in your reader's mind. Identify all possible readers and get your focus adjusted to theirs. Echo the reader.

Know Your Product

Let's look again at the three major ways you can build persuasion into a report. An effective, persuasive report differs from an "ordinary" report in the following ways:

1. *The report's conclusions and recommendations come first, before the supporting details.* This is perhaps the most important service you can render your readers: to tell them up front what the results of your research are. That is what all report readers want to know, no matter who they are.

You'll offer supporting details in a later section for those who want to know more. And a section at the very end of the report can contain some of the original source material for readers who want the most complete picture.

Don't worry; you don't have to write the conclusions first. When you're finished writing the report, you'll rearrange it that way to echo the reader's needs.

2. *The report contains some planned repetition.* Like a news story, reports should be organized to offer the reader fast comprehension. This entails a little repetition as you move through the report, recapping what you've already said. Put summaries in the introduction, in the discussion section, and at the end. This allows the reader to read quickly, yet not miss anything.

3. *The report has a clear, easy-to-follow organization.* This means that a skimming reader can leaf through the report and find what she's looking for fast. You'll use clear visual signals—headings, underlining, listings, and a good table of contents—to make this possible.

Stick to One Big Idea

Take the simple statement of purpose you wrote down before you began analyzing your audience. This will serve as a guide to the main idea of your report, the peg on which everything else will be hung.

Because reports are longer than letters or memos, they especially need the One Big Idea focus to keep the reader alert to what you're getting at through pages of data and supporting information. And it will keep reminding you of what's relevant to include and what's not.

For example, if your purpose statement is *"To find the causes of absenteeism on the first shift in the Hartford plant and recommend ways to correct it,"* your One Big Idea is going to be the cause of and cure for this problem. You may not be able to say what these are as you begin your research, but the framework will keep you focused while you analyze the data.

When you've finished your research and are ready to write, your One Big Idea may look like this: *"The 20 percent absentee rate on the first shift at the Hartford plant is caused by lack of supervision; to correct it, we need to draft new procedures for keeping track of attendance."*

Your One Big Idea will focus for you both the research and the writing process for the report in a time-saving way. And, properly emphasized in the written report, it will keep detail in a manageable framework for the reader.

How much research? Reports may be based on company records, laboratory experiments, market testing, surveys, questionnaires, travel to a site, interviews, actual library research, even personal observation. The method you use will depend, of course, on your subject.

But how much research will be required? Here are some guidelines:

- Using your audience analysis, determine the scope of the report—how much it needs to cover—and the amount of research required to present the subject adequately for your readers' levels of knowledge.
- Be sure that you have explored *all* the possible sources of information for your report.
- Gather all the information you need *before* you start to write.

As we've seen, if your audience is already very familiar with your subject, your task is easier; you won't have to fill in much of the history or supplemental details of the situation for them. But if, for example, you're doing a report on marketing prospects for your company's new wine cooler in Alaska, everything about the subject may be entirely new to your readers, and you'll have to include substantial background to convince them of your conclusions.

What to report? Your purpose statement will help you decide what research material is relevant and what isn't. Be ruthless about relevance; it will pay off in the writing and keep you from time-wasting digressions.

The structure of reports includes a place for an appendix, where extra source material of interest only to those readers who want the full story, or who like to see tables and charts, can go. Include here any material you think fills out your findings but isn't directly related to your main point.

You'll need to devise some systematic method for compiling your research: using legal pads, perhaps; a copying machine; a tape recorder; or even a computer. Still very effective for note taking are the standard 3- by 5-inch index cards. Jot down information or copy quotations on one side only. The card method works well when you begin to organize the report, since you can physically arrange the cards on a table or desk in piles or sequence to give you an idea of the major divisions of the report.

The research end of report writing is a matter of thorough and accurate reporting, something on which the ultimate credibility of the entire report depends. Be scrupulous about crediting sources, checking figures, using exact quotations, and spelling all names correctly as you conduct your research.

Know Your Subject

Let's assume that you've already done the basic research for a report, assigned to you by your boss, assessing the possibilities for opening a new branch office in another state. You've tracked down the vital statistics on the proposed location and its markets, researched other businesses that have opened offices there, even visited the site yourself and talked to people who live and work in the area.

You know your subject. The most credible reports are based on such thorough knowledge. The sense of authority that comes from knowing what you're talking about gives your writing a convincing edge. And, most of the time, the so-called writer's block is really a matter of not knowing enough about a subject.

That's why it's important to get all the information you need *before* you start to write. This is bound to give you momentum when you do begin, and will save you valuable time during the writing process.

Organize for Understanding

A business report structure that's already in fairly common use will save you time in organizing persuasively. You should check to see whether your own company has a model it prefers for reports; if not, the following basic organization is well-accepted and useful. Moreover, it offers the kind of fast reading and understanding that persuasion requires. Note that the order in which the components of the finished report are arranged, for the reader's use, is different from the order in which you, the writer, will write them. You'll begin writing the report at No. 5 and rearrange the components later.

1. A title page. Like the memo, a report should have a good title to alert the reader to its subject and pique his interest. Avoid too-general titles, like "Absenteeism." Instead, "How to Solve the Problem of Employee Absenteeism at the Hartford Plant" would be much more informative and interesting.

The title page should also include your name and title, the date, and any other information required to identify the report within the company.

2. A table of contents. The table of contents serves as an important guide and overview for the reader, indicating the major sections of the report, and if you wish, all the subdivisions as well. Here again, use good titles; you can take them directly from the subheadings you've used in the finished report.

3. *Your conclusions and recommendations.* It comes as a surprise to most writers that they must put the end first in a report. Of course, you can't *write* the conclusions first; you'll simply rearrange the finished report for the reader's best use.

This up-front summary is basically the Good News format you're already familiar with. Busy readers want to know what your results are, and putting these first is very helpful to them.

As we'll see shortly, there are some report situations where you shouldn't present your conclusions first, The Bad News format is more appropriate when your conclusions or recommendations may disappoint the reader.

4. *Introduction.* The introduction should be a one-page statement of the purpose of the report, your methods of research, the scope of the report, and a summary of your findings.

5. *Discussion.* In the main and longest section of your report, you'll present your findings in detail, analyze data, and offer background if necessary. You should write this section first.

It should be made easy to read, with subheadings, underlining, short paragraphs, and a style accessible to all readers.

6. *Graphs and charts.* The best place for graphs and charts is right in the discussion section of the report, placed wherever you're talking about them. But some companies prefer to have them grouped at the end in their own separate section.

7. *Appendix* (optional). Any source material—tables, statistics, excerpts from other reports—you think pertinent for further understanding of the report belongs in the appendix.

8. *References and footnotes* (optional). Ideally, you'll work all your references into the body of the report as you discuss them. For example, *"As H. R. Kirk, president of XYZ Corporation, told executives at the Annual Marketing Society Meeting in April . . ."*

However, you may wish to add reference material at the end to bolster your credibility and to show the reader where to find additional information.

A good and accepted shortcut for footnote/bibliography references is one used in technical writing. Alphabetize your sources and number them in a list titled "References." Then, after a reference in the body of the report, use the number you've assigned the source in your list. Add a colon and the page numbers from which the material was taken and enclose in parentheses: *The results of the test marketing in Cleveland showed that products labeled 'New' outsold all others by a margin of three to one (4:36–7).*

The number 4 in your parenthetical footnote is the number you've assigned to the book in your alphabetized list; the other numbers are the exact pages on which this information can be found. The system eliminates the need for any formal footnotes and makes reference material easy for the reader to find.

Choose the Right Format

The biggest problem in writing reports is organizing them. But by using one of the three basic formats for persuasion, you'll find this stage much easier. You can even eliminate the need for a detailed report outline.

The only section of the report that will need special organizing is the discussion section. It will be the first part you write. The remaining sections of the report—the introduction and conclusion, for example—can be written later. By then, you'll find that you know exactly what to say and can handle them in a page or two.

The Good News format. The Good News format offers the best structure for reports. It satisfies the reader's curiosity by putting the most important information—in this case, your findings and your recommendations—up front. And because not every reader will need to know everything about your topic, this structure allows the individual reader to decide how much further to read.

Although your entire report will be organized according to the inverted pyramid of the Good News format, the discussion section itself must also be designed with a good summary at the beginning. But, obviously, you won't be able to start *writing* the section that way.

Instead, start by dividing the discussion section itself into the three-part Good News structure. Your actual writing will begin with the middle (see Figure 3–1), the data and explanation of details you yourself have been analyzing in your research. Begin organizing this middle portion of your discussion by making a list of all the points you need to present, in any order (the brainstorming technique).

Ordering the details. Now, number the points according to priority. If the problem you're solving has a clear *cause-effect sequence,* number your points to suit that sequence. Or if it has a *chronological order,* number them that way.

The most persuasive order for this portion of your report is the *or-*

der of familiarity, beginning with the details the reader already knows. This connects with what's already in the reader's head, establishing a link between what the reader accepts as reliable information and the new information or ideas you're going to introduce.

A variation of this is the *order of acceptance,* where you present first the details you know your readers will agree with, then the more controversial material.

Now, make a scratch outline and write the middle of the discussion section according to the order you've chosen. As you complete this portion of the report, you'll find yourself moving naturally toward some conclusions about the problem you've been studying and discovering ways to solve it.

When you've finished writing the discussion section, your conclusions and recommendations will be transposed to a separate page at the very beginning of the report. According to the inverted pyramid structure of the Good News format, you should also summarize them at the beginning of the discussion section.

Writing the introduction. When the major work of explaining the details of your report is completed, you'll be in a much better position to write a succinct introduction for the report. This will contain four subheadings:

Purpose: A one-paragraph statement of why the report was written
Method: A description of the way research for the report was done
Scope: What the report covers and in how much detail
Summary: A brief overview of the contents of the report

The Bad News format. Since the Bad News format follows more naturally the actual process of your own writing, you may find the Bad News structure easier to use for reports. However, you should use it only when your conclusions or recommendations will be controversial or disappointing to your readers.

Although it offers a better psychological way to present bad news, the structure of the Bad News format delays the most important information in the report in order to prepare the reader. Thus, what precedes it has to be interesting enough so as not to tax the reader's patience.

Again, begin with the discussion section of the report. The best method of organizing your data when you have bad news is to use the order of acceptance. Present the material you know the reader will agree with first (the you-section of the Bad News format—see Figure 3–3).

Then, work into the controversial material or bad news by explaining the reasons for it first, as in the second segment of the Bad News format. The details may be organized within this segment any way you choose: in a cause-effect or chronological sequence or in the order of familiarity or acceptance.

Finally, present the bad news. By this time, the reader will be prepared for it because you've already given the details that explain it.

At the end of the discussion section, don't repeat the bad news. Instead, build support for your conclusions by reinforcing benefits and talking about the positive aspects of your findings.

This is the only kind of report where you won't place your conclusions and recommendations at the beginning. Instead, you'll move in natural order right after the table of contents to an introduction and into the discussion section, eliminating the separate opening page of conclusions.

Psychologically, this is the only way to gain support for your findings without putting your readers on the defensive. Angry or upset readers are difficult to persuade. If they get the bad news too soon, they may never read the rest of the report to find out how you arrived at your conclusions.

The AIM format. The AIM format will help you put real "sell" into a report. The AIM structure offers you a framework for building motivation that will be especially helpful in developing confidence in what you say and winning support for your recommendations. Use it whenever you're proposing new systems, suggesting changes, and promoting your ideas—or whenever you need to capture a disinterested or resistant group of readers.

Within this format, you must decide, based on your reader analysis, whether to present your conclusions and recommendations first. If they are surprising or controversial, it would be more persuasive to present them *after* you've built up attention and interest.

Use the AIM format primarily to organize the discussion section of your report (see Figure 3–5):

A *stands for attention.* Begin with a strong echo of your readers' concerns. The you-approach always gets attention. Or begin with a "grabber": a question, an announcement, a quotation. A very good grabber for business reports is a reference to the company's history. For example: *"In 1890, when XYZ Corporation was just a one-room office with two employees, the company was already doing business on an international level."*

I *stands for interest.* You build interest in any proposition by offering benefits for adopting it. You should outline for your readers the ways in which their jobs will be improved and their responsibilities lessened, or describe how the company's business will improve because of what you're proposing. It's here, after you've described the benefits, that you can most convincingly present your conclusions. Save the recommendations for your call to action.

M *stands for motivation.* Give ample evidence—statistics, testimonials, test-market results—that what you're advocating is worth your reader's confidence and acceptance. Objectivity and thoroughness in presenting these data will mean the most in motivating your audience. This is a place not for the hard sell, but for a complete demonstration of the convincing facts that have led to your conclusion.

In the call to action, present your recommendations as the suggested solution to the problem or method of proceeding.

Find the Central Selling Point

Whatever your subject, you should always find a Central Selling Point for it, just as a way of keeping your own focus on persuasive strategy as you write. This selling point, with its emphasis on benefits, will also help you convince readers of the value of your idea and show them why it's the best one.

Remember the procedure: pick out the unique or most important feature of your subject, problem, or proposition and match it to a benefit for the reader. Use your main idea, and pair it with a description of its benefits. It's easy to do this when you're writing about a business problem. Simply match the problem to its solution as a ready-made selling point, emphasizing a benefit of the solution: *"The most cost-efficient way to stop absenteeism on the first shift is to design a new system for keeping track of attendance and appoint someone to supervise it."*

In reports, the best way to use a selling point is to turn the whole report into an argument for your own position on the subject: *"If we sell the wine cooler as an exotic drink rather than as just another calorie-conscious soda pop, we will have a chance to capture the big market of Alaskan customers who are thirsty for variety and excitement."*

Taking a stand and making your main point into an argument will energize your report and make it easier for you to organize and write.

Remember to build your case on benefits. And sell use. Describe and dramatize for the reader the way your proposition will work in his own office or as he puts it into practice: *"This new system of keeping track of attendance will eliminate the need for daily reports and allow additional time for more important tasks."*

A Central Selling Point for any report: the promise of a fast read and a clear main idea.

Adopt a Conservative Style

The most persuasive report style is one that has a tone of objectivity. This supports the sense that what you're saying is impartial and fair. Being objective doesn't, however, mean being impersonal. Your acknowledgement of the reader on the other side of the page is always important to her acceptance of what you say.

However, the style you use for reports should be slightly more formal than your letter or memo style. You can accomplish this in two ways without losing any of the ease and naturalness you've already learned to add to your style:

1. Eliminate contractions.
2. Don't address the reader directly as "you."

Contractions are an immediate way to give a conversational flavor to what you write. Because of their informality, they may seem too breezy to some report readers, implying that what you say is less than serious; it's better simply to avoid them.

Directly addressing the reader may imply too much familiarity, an assumption some readers may find offensive. Be conservative in reports and keep some distance for objectivity.

Contrary to popular belief, it's permissible to use "I" in more formal writing, especially when the alternative is awkward, like "this writer." You're the expert on the subject, after all, and a statement that you make about it has some authority. It's also permissible, and a good idea, to use the personal pronouns "we" and "our" in speaking about the company. This helps credibility in the presentation of data. Once again, however, there's a happy medium between a style that's too stiff and one that's too chatty.

Any style, for example, that makes what you say hard to understand or awkward to phrase is too formal: *The writer wishes to note that, these circumstances notwithstanding, it is of utmost importance that the proposition be implemented for immediate application in the company's Hartford plant.* This would be clearer in more natural and familiar words: *Extra supervision and a new attendance system are needed immediately at our Hartford plant.*

A report style that is too informal, exaggerated, or hard selling may put the reader off: *You'll find you can hardly wait to try this new marketing method I'm suggesting. It knocked the socks off 'em in Cincinnati.*

In reports, *do* continue to write as you talk. But keep your style on the conservative side by eliminating contractions and not addressing the reader directly.

Talk the Reader's Language

If your report requires the use of special terminology or shoptalk, be sure that your readers understand it. Scientific language is fine if yours is, say, an audience of chemists. But if, for example, your report on the test results of a new plastic is going to the board of directors for approval, you must translate for the nonspecialist.

Using clear, familiar words will guarantee that everyone who reads the report will understand it without having to look up the meanings of words. Any time that you slow the reader down with a hard-to-understand vocabulary, you risk losing his interest.

There are certain words, particularly scientific terms, that don't translate or have synonyms. If you must use them, provide a small glossary at the end of your report where you define any terms the layperson may not know.

Remember that people like to get information in the easiest way possible; you shouldn't make them work hard to figure out what you mean.

Be Positive

As in all other written persuasion, the positive approach is more easily accepted and remembered than a negative one. Couch negatives in a positive way. Say "We wish it were possible" rather than "We cannot"; say "I see a future for us in plastics" rather than "I don't see any future for us in ceramics"; say "It should be easy to put this plan into operation" rather than "I hope we won't have any difficulty putting this plan into operation."

It's possible to go overboard with this and undermine the reader's sense of your objectivity, however. It's always disarming to admit to a small weakness here and there, especially if the rest of what you're saying builds a good case; readers will trust you more if you acknowledge some minor drawbacks occasionally.

Paint the Picture with Colorful Nouns and Active Verbs

Being objective does *not* mean being abstract. A vocabulary of abstract words leaves readers with no sense of the reality behind what you say, and leaves too much room for misunderstanding.

Whenever possible, bring your writing down to the concrete, tangible world with nouns that name real things. Say "Dagwood Tool" instead of "the corporation"; say "an extra $100,000 a year" instead of "profit"; say "December 10" instead of "a few months from now."

Be as precise in the words you use as you would be about the integrity of your data. When, for example, is the word "further" preferable to "farther"? When is "affect" used instead of "effect"? "Principle" instead of "principal"? Your goal is to remain in control of the meaning of what you say, so that your readers don't misunderstand.

Watch out, as always, for the deadening effects of the passive verb. The passive provides a handy way to pass the buck, but only if you're using it deliberately for that purpose. Otherwise, it merely saps the energy in a sentence: *"The drop in attendance was noticed by the district manager."* Maintaining the natural word order of English from "actor" to "act" to "action" is better: *The district manager noticed the drop in attendance.*

Use Short Sentences and Paragraphs

Because reports are longer than letters and memos, it's doubly important that they be easy to read. The best sentence length for any business writing is between 17 and 22 words. Of course, you can and should vary sentence length.

Use short paragraphs, as well, to increase reading speed. It *is* permissible to use one-sentence paragraphs, especially when you want to emphasize an important point. Frequent paragraph breaks offer pauses in eye movement for the reader and encourage further reading.

Use Visual Effects for Reader Appeal

Make the organization of your report easy to understand and visually clear.

Headings and Subheadings. Frequent breaks in your text will not only make it look easier to read but also make it easier for readers to follow and to find the information they're most interested in.

Like little titles throughout your report, headings and subheadings make writing easier by eliminating the need for transitions between topics. Instead of having to provide links like "moreover" or "in addition," you can use subheadings to do the job.

Position headings and subheadings prominently for the reader's use. Capitalize major subheadings, such as INTRODUCTION, DISCUSSION, CONCLUSIONS; underline them; and center them at the beginning of a section.

To divide the text further, position a second level of subheadings at the left margin, capitalizing the first letter of major words and underlining, like this: Purpose.

A third level of headings in the text can be centered at the beginning of the material you wish to mark.

Further subdivisions in the text can be marked as follows:

- At the beginning of a paragraph:

  Need for new system. Keeping a record of attendance reminds employees of its importance. . . .

- Or at the beginning of a sentence:

  Keeping a record of attendance reminds employees of its importance. . . .

White Space. The picture your reader gets of your report at first glance is worth a thousand of its words. It should look neat, professional, and easy to read.

Good use of blank space, or "white" space as it's called, frames your text for the eye and gives the promise of effortless reading.

Don't try to save paper; ask whoever is typing your report to double-space the text and to leave at least a 1-inch margin at the top, bottom, and sides of each page. Leave a 1-inch space before and after subheadings as well, to make them stand out.

Graphics. Graphs, charts, pictures, and other visual examples of what you're saying bring your subject to life for readers faster than words. Search for ways to illustrate what you're saying, in simple bar graphs or condensed charts. The kinds used in annual reports are a good example, simplified to allow quick understanding of major points in the text.

More detailed tables and charts can be appended to the report for readers who need further information.

Rules for Short Reports

The report formats and techniques discussed here can be applied to shorter reports, such as progress and periodic reports and proposals.

Choose the structural components that will make your short report easy to read. You won't need a table of contents, for example, in very short reports. And you can devise some combination of the three major report sections for your purposes, perhaps with a one-paragraph introduction, a short discussion, and a separate page of conclusions and/or recommendations placed at the beginning (if bad news, at the end).

The memo format, with its TO, FROM, and SUBJECT headings, is also appropriate for most short reports. Simple and streamlined, it offers a familiar framework that's easy for readers to follow. Use one of the persuasive formats within it to provide the best structure for your material.

Sample Report Structure

The next few pages contain an excerpt from a report (Figure 8–1). This fictitious report is presented to give you an idea of how to organize and use each section of a standard business report.

Figure 8–1.   Sample report structure.

HOW TO SELL A WINE COOLER IN ALASKA

By J. Biffington Furbes
Marketing Manager

XYZ CORPORATION

December 10, 1986

TABLE
OF
CONTENTS

CONCLUSIONS
AND
RECOMMENDATIONS

Conclusions

We will be going into the Alaskan market with virtually no competition and the advantage of being first with a wine cooler.

Although the typical customer is unfamiliar with this kind of beverage, he is interested in variety and in new products. Our initial test marketing showed that selling the wine cooler as a lighter, diet drink is not as effective as positioning it as a different, new wine with a better taste.

A marketing campaign conducted in Anchorage would reach enough potential customers to launch word-of-mouth interest in other parts of the state. The prospects for substantial sales in the first year are excellent.

Recommendations

I recommend the following steps to market Vinofino in Alaska:

1. Position it as a serious drink with a new taste, not a diet soda pop.
2. Conduct a news and broadcast advertising campaign in Anchorage, supplemented by billboard announcements and point-of-purchase placards and giveaways in restaurants and bars.
3. Get there first; launch the campaign by June 1st to hit hardest during the summer months.

INTRODUCTION

Purpose

The purpose of this report is to explore the prospects for selling XYZ Corporation's new wine cooler in Alaska.

Alaska offers a great untapped market for new products, particularly beverages. Most companies, however, have been unwilling to invest in full-scale product launching where it is so difficult to target an audience.

Yet, as this report will show, a well-timed promotional campaign with thorough media coverage can give a product such as ours an enormous, fast exposure in Alaska and build brand awareness in a remarkably short time.

Method

This report is based on marketing surveys by Sell 'Em, Inc. and on 1986 demographic studies conducted in Alaska by Populace Corp.

Research on promotional campaigns and product launches done by XYZ's Marketing Department provided valuable background for designing an Alaska launch plan for our wine cooler.

Scope

The report includes a brief history of marketing efforts for beverages in Alaska, along with case studies of successful and lackluster product launches over the past 10 years. It summarizes population growth studies done during this century and includes an analysis of sales figures for alcoholic beverages from 1965–1985.

Summary

The report begins with background information on the Alaskan populace, terrain, and living conditions. It tracks the marketing of alcoholic beverages in the state, revealing the best locales for marketing. In the United States, there is a growing demand for wine coolers, especially among females. The report describes wine-cooler marketing and demonstrates how foreign competitors—Japan, Australia, Canada, and Ireland—have made inroads on this market. Surveying demographic and sales studies, the report offers strategies for a June 1987 product launch in Anchorage.

DISCUSSION

Demographics

Most of Alaska's nearly 400,000 people live in or near the city of Anchorage (46 percent in 1980) (6), where bars are more numerous than churches. The remaining population is largely concentrated in Alaska's Panhandle region around the state capital, Juneau, with a smattering in the interior surrounding Fairbanks. Small pockets of people have settled in tiny villages, though the Arctic plains, the Bering shores, and the Aleutians remain sparsely populated (2:412).

Contrary to popular opinion, Alaska is not full of aborigines. Only about one-seventh of the population is made up of Eskimos, Aleuts, and Indians (2:411), and since 1950 more than 100,000 people have immigrated to the forty-ninth state, making it a melting pot of American, Russian, Japanese, Chinese, Filipino, and other nationalities. Of the state's current population, some 80,000 people are American military personnel and their families.

A Frontier Life

Though the ratio of males to females (5-to-1 in the early part of the century) is nearing equality, frontier conditions persist. The Alaska terrain is still largely Arctic wilderness where temperatures drop as low as -34 degrees C during the long winter. The cost of living is the highest in the United States, keeping labor and transportation expenses high and outside investors at bay.

REFERENCES

1. Banker, H.H., *History of Alaska* (Anchorage: *Gold, Inc.,* 1959).
2. *Encyclopedia Britannica,* 15th edition, vol. 1 (Chicago: Encyclopedia Brittanica, Inc., 1980).
3. Ferringer, S.C., *Moonlight at Midday* (New York: Random House, 1960).
4. Populace Corp., "A Demographic Study of the 49th State" (1986).
5. Sell 'Em, Inc. "Alaska Marketing Survey," (July 1986).
6. U.S. Census Bureau Report, 1980.

Chapter Nine

Writing Sales Letters that Do the Job

Sales letters are the one kind of business writing in which persuasive tactics can have full sway. You can concentrate totally on selling. And the more your letter involves the reader, the more successful it will be, just as an engaging salesperson can do better on the selling floor than one who shows no interest in the customer.

Actually, the sales letter has an advantage over selling in person because you can be in complete control of what you say and have time to think and plan it all out in advance.

Persuasion Power

It's personal. The sales letter is persuasive because it arrives as a personal message, addressed to customers by name and in their mailboxes. You can't beat that for a door-to-door campaign.

It goes to the right customers. Whether it is written to one person or as a form letter sent to a list of customers, the sales letter has more AIM than a magazine advertisement, a television commercial, or even a person-to-person sale. It can go directly to customers already targeted as prospects for a product, service, or idea. You don't waste time talking to the wrong customer or to a very diversified audience.

It measures results. And, with a sales letter, you can keep track of the results your message gets. You'll know how persuasive it is by the number of replies it pulls. Even a department store cash register can't gauge the pulling power of an ad that accurately.

It's an inexpensive way to sell. Overall, the sales letter is one of the least expensive ways to sell. It's a real door-to-door campaign without all the hassle of ringing doorbells.

Sales letters save time and money because they target just the right prospects, go to all of them, and make a well-organized, personal sales pitch right in the customer's own home or office.

It's versatile. Use the sales letter to sell a new product or an ongoing service, to drum up trade in new sales territory, to create goodwill among existing customers, or to support your dealers out in the field. You can use sales letter techniques in drafting proposals and writing grant applications, too. The sales letter is a useful, flexible selling tool for whatever you have in mind.

It's easier. People like to buy things through the mail if the phenomenal success of catalog and direct-mail sales in the last decade is any indication. It's easier. They can pick their own time, and they can make decisions at leisure without leaving the house or the office. They can browse without pressure from a salesperson, and since all the product information—including price—is right in front of them, they don't have to ask questions or go looking for anything.

That's persuasive in itself. The sales letter puts decision making into the customers' hands—literally—which is where they like it to be.

It's designed to sell. Persuasion can be as powerful on paper as in person when you know how to target your audience, organize your message, and marshal your words for selling. Having read this far into the book, you already know how to do these things and perhaps have tested them out in your own business writing. Now you'll need everything you've learned so far. Every element of the sales letter, from the envelope to the postscript, must be designed to sell.

Special Tactics for the Sales Letter

Sales letters are costly only if the message doesn't persuade the reader to buy. Such a letter will wind up in the wastebasket faster than you can say "junk mail." Without a smiling salesperson on hand to coax and cajole, the sales letter is on its own to get the customer's attention, hold it long enough for persuasion to take effect, and create the right climate for action.

Although you don't want to tamper with the sales letter's image as a personal letter, you can take creative chances with it that will increase its persuasive power and invite customers to read. To get your message across, you have to use an imaginative design, good attention-getters, and a clear offer.

Customers are bombarded these days with letters and catalogs trying to sell them something. The competition's keen because selling by mail is so effective. Everybody's getting into the act. A sales letter has to go out of its way to attract attention, just to keep from being lumped in with all the rest.

Your imagination and creativity will come in handy to help your message stand out. But, first, you have to get the customer to open the envelope.

Start Your Message on the Envelope

Sales letters can set themselves apart from the rest by the appearance of the envelope. Slogans, questions, see-through windows, and announcements printed on the outside tempt customers to open the envelope.

To get the kind of attention your message needs, start your message on the envelope. An announcement, a provocative quotation or statement, a small gift inside, or a coupon will invite the customer to open the envelope.

The best and easiest method is to use a "grabber," an attention-getting phrase, question, or slogan that arouses the customer's curiosity. Here are some suggestions:

1. *Use the you-approach:*
   You're on our list.
   For our preferred customers only.
   We'd like to make you a millionaire.

2. *Make a promise:*
   You may already have won $1,000,000!
   Save 50 percent on your next carpet purchase.
   Earn money in your spare time.

3. *Arouse curiosity with a question or teaser:*
   MOXIE: Find Out How Much You've Got.
   What's the one thing every woman should know about men?
   There *is* a cure for cancer.

4. *Use an incomplete or split sentence:*
   Thank you.
   Before you sell your house . . .
   Open at once.
   Announcing . . .

5. *Use a quotation that relates to your message:*
   For those to whom much is given, much is required.
                                                    —John F. Kennedy
   Come up and see me sometime.
                                                    —Mae West
   All I know is just what I read in the papers.
                                                    —Will Rogers

Of course, you'll key the "grabber" to your specific product. And you'll keep it short and simple. The message on the envelope is like a headline on a news story: it must get to the point, be easy to read, and interest the reader in what's to come.

Another good way to get the envelope opened is to make the sales letter look as much like a personal letter as possible. Use a handwritten address, a postage stamp instead of a meter mark, and no printing (not even a return address) on the envelope. It looks personal, and may get opened automatically.

Get the Customer Reading

Once your customer's reading, it's as good as the proverbial salesperson's foot in the door. At least your message has a chance to take effect. The sales letter should look easy to read, with lots of white space, short words, short sentences, and frequent paragraphs (one-sentence paragraphs can add special emphasis in the sales letter).

Oddly enough, the most successful sales letters tend to be longer than the average business letter. Once your customer is hooked, she likes to read about what she'll get, savoring description and details. But since your sales letter can be longer than most letters you write, it has to be designed especially well for visual appeal and easy reading.

Use a headline. Sales letters can depart from the norm in significant ways to get attention and get the customer reading. One way is to use headlines, a kind of special effect to provide visual interest and emphasis. Headlines can be used all the way through the letter to focus on key points.

Use a headline—a "grabber"—at the top of your letter, as in Figure 9–1. Here are some other examples:

You can take a Caribbean cruise this winter for under $395.
Now you can own the car you've always dreamed about.
Here's one offer you can't refuse . . .

Figure 9–1. Using the AIM format in a sales letter.

Use an above-the-line headline.	SWEET-TALK HER WITH MINERVA CHOCOLATES
Attention: you-approach	When you want to tell her she's special, there's nothing that says it better than a one-of-a-kind box of our hand-dipped chocolates.
Interest: match features with benefits	Every piece is carefully coated, by hand, in chocolate so rich she'll wonder if it's legal. At the center, she'll find all kinds of surprises—fresh almonds, creamy mints, velvety caramels, sweet liqueurs. All wrapped, one at a time, in thick gold paper.
Motivation: "prove" with facts	Because we import our own cocoa beans and get our cream and fresh butter from local dairies, we can afford to make chocolate that is probably the richest you've ever tasted. The recipe is a secret, but we can tell you it's been in the family for three generations and nobody's been able to duplicate it—though they've tried.
Call to action: suggest action and a benefit of action	If your love life's been a little sour lately, pick up a box of these very special chocolates on your way home tonight and let Minerva do your sweet-talking for you. She'll get the message.

Try a headline just after the salutation to rivet attention on a key point. Headlines can be emphatic at the end of the letter as well, focusing on your offer or the call to action.

Get attention in the first paragraph. In the sales letter, the first paragraph is all-important. It must welcome the reader, get his attention, and invite him to read on. The basic AIM format provides for this with an attention-getting, reader-oriented beginning. Here are two good examples:

> You don't want to hang around again this winter while all your friends are in warm places. Right now, you could book passage on a luxury liner and spend January soaking up the sun—and at half the price your friends are paying.

> You've waited a long time for the chance to own your own home. Now that the interest rates on our new Adjusto-Rate mortgage have come down, this could be the time to make your move.

A series of one-sentence paragraphs can entice the reader into the sales letter, too. She'll have to read two or three of them just to get started; by then, she may be close enough to the middle to finish the letter, just out of a natural desire to finish what she started or out of sheer curiosity:

> Dear Cardholder:

> You've probably noticed people using a new Sapphire Card when you've been out in the restaurants and theatres lately.

> Maybe you've wondered what they've got that you haven't got—and how to get it.

> Now you can enjoy Sapphire Card privileges of instant recognition, cash advances, and credit that announce you as a Number One Customer wherever you go.

And so on. The tactic will compel the reader to keep going. And the method is simple: don't put all the ideas in one paragraph. Carry them along in a series of one-sentence paragraphs, each offering a benefit or a bit of suspense.

Keep the Customer Reading

Use visual appeals. As we've said, the sales letter looks different from other kinds of business letters because it sells *visually,* too, to get attention. The better it looks, the better it will sell.

For example, you should consider other materials for the sales letter besides the standard (and conservative) executive bond paper. Papers of different colors and textures attract attention, convey an image, and motivate buyers. You might consider using an off-white envelope to make your letter stand out in the rest of the white-paper mail. Or a glossy finish to give your letter polish. Or a heavy, textured paper to lend weight to your sales talk.

On the other hand, it may be that a low-key approach will go over best with your particular audience, and you'll decide deliberately to use the standard business letter approach.

To alert the reader that your message is out of the ordinary, consider these possibilities:

- Use a headline before the salutation to draw attention.
- Use different kinds of type to emphasize different points.
- Use subheadings to break the text into small, easy-to-read segments.
- Underline for emphasis.
- Use a list like this to set off special points.
- Add a postscript to highlight your offer (everyone reads the P.S.).
- Use enclosures. A free gift, a handwritten note, a coupon, a pre-addressed and stamped envelope for replies, or a trial offer can lend support to your sales message in customer-pleasing ways.

The AT&T sales letter in Figure 9–2 illustrates an effective use of visual appeals—headlines, special typography, and a postscript—to attract attention and emphasize important points.

If your company has its own in-house art department, ask for advice on making sales letters visually appealing. You can also consult outside firms that specialize in mass mailings and can suggest papers, typefaces, and layouts. They can also handle the actual mailing for you.

Look at your own daily allotment of sales letters to see what works and what doesn't. Consider the image you'd like to project, and collect ideas that appeal to you.

Even though imagination helps in the sales letter, be wary of being too innovative. It can put customers off and undermine your credibility. Understatement, whether in words or graphics, is usually more convincing. Stick with the basic letter format, but work to give it visual interest and a readable design.

Remember: a sales letter is a letter. One of the biggest selling points about the sales letter is its familiar and personal appeal as a letter. Al-

Figure 9–2. A sales letter sells visually.

Introducing AT&T's Reach Out™ America Plan. . .

NOW, NO MATTER HOW FAR YOU CALL, SAVINGS AND QUALITY LONG DISTANCE SERVICE ARE WITHIN REACH!

Dear AT&T Customer:

Now, when you make calls outside your state, AT&T can help you get more high-quality long distance service at affordable prices . . . with the introduction of our "Reach Out" America plan.

"Reach Out" America is a new way to buy long distance. Unlike anything you've known in the past. That's because the plan is based on time, not distance. So, you only pay by the hour, not by the mile!

> With the "Reach Out" America plan, you can buy an hour's worth of direct-dialed weekend and night state-to-state calls to any part of the United States—including Alaska, Hawaii, Puerto Rico and the U.S. Virgin Islands—for a low hourly rate.

You'll have the freedom to call more . . . and talk longer. Because the time is yours to use as you like! For example, you can make one 60-minute call . . . or two 30-minute calls . . . even six 10-minute calls. No matter how you divide the time, it's all included in the low hourly rate!

What's more, the "Reach Out" America plan gives you greater control over your monthly long distance costs. Because you can always know—in advance—what those costs will be.

We've enclosed a brochure that clearly outlines all the benefits of the AT&T "Reach Out" America plan. Once you read it, we think you'll agree that only AT&T can offer you the high-quality long distance service that counts . . . at affordable rates you can count on!

Sincerely,

A. T. Rep
AT&T "Reach Out" Services

P.S. If you act <u>now</u>, you'll be able to save—because we'll waive the
regular $10 order processing charge. So take a look at the
brochure, then send us your enrollment card right away. Or, for
even faster service, call, toll-free: 1 800 551-3131.

though any departure from this norm has an immediate, attention-getting effect, it's best to preserve the elements that say "letter": the inside address, the salutation, the complimentary close, and the personal signature.

But you can jazz these up, too, primarily by making them as personal as possible. The best attention-getter is always the customer's own name and address. Computers have streamlined the process of writing form letters so well that the insertion of names and addresses looks authentic.

Sometimes, however, a general salutation will be more appropriate, to let a customer know he's part of a select group: "Dear Cardholder"; "Dear Pontiac Owner"; "Dear Professor."

Consider also who should sign the letter. The signature and title of an important member of your organization can add authority and authenticity. Perhaps it should be the CEO, or the sales manager, or even a celebrity who will endorse the product.

Make Them an Offer

Because everything in a sales letter is geared for a sale, the customer's purchase decision should be made as simple and appealing as possible.

This is accomplished by the "offer," an extra deal you make with your reader. It could be a discount price, a free trial, a money-back-if-you're-not-satisfied guarantee, or some other persuasive reason to buy.

Car dealers, for example, know the value of an offer. After they've shown you the car, taken you out for a test drive, and explained special features, they'll offer you a deal to motivate the sale.

The offer in the sales letter has the same purpose. It's an extra inducement to act. The offer is usually added on near the end of the sales letter, after you've described the product and built motivation for it. Then it becomes part of what's called "closing the sale," the clincher that ensures action.

Note the way *Psychology Today* made its subscription offer*:

> *Send no money.* Our magazine is $1.95 a copy on newsstands. But when you send back the enclosed card promptly, you'll receive the new issue free, with our compliments. No cost. No obligation. No strings. Look it over. Share it with the family. Enjoy it from cover to cover.
>
> *Free issue.* If it's not for you, just return the subscription invoice marked "cancel" within two weeks, and that's that. You've spent nothing. You owe nothing. You're under no further obligation. And the issue is yours to keep.

However, the offer you're planning to make should be one of the first elements you think about in writing the sales letter. Present it in a simple, emphatic way:

> *Look the coverage over for 30 days with no obligation. Send no money.*
> *Order now. Pay later.*
> *If you're not satisfied that everything we've said about Gizmo-Gadget is true, simply return it and we'll refund your money.*
> *With any $10 purchase, you'll get a special bonus bottle of Eau de Parfum absolutely free.*

Anything you can do to visually emphasize your offer will help—underlining, single-sentence paragraphs, color, typography. However, it's essentially the way you phrase it that makes an offer enticing. For example, which of the offers below would you choose?

1. Buy now and get a discount.
2. You'll get a 25 percent discount if you buy before Christmas.
3. This book will cost you 25 percent *more* if you buy after Christmas.
4. You'll save $10 if you order before December 15.

* Used by permission.

The more specific and reader-oriented offer, the one that tells the reader exactly what the offer is and what he'll get, works best. Here, it's No. 4.

Strategy for the Sales Letter

With all its creative options, the sales letter still depends on the same basic strategies as all persuasive business writing. So, plan the sales letter by using the steps of Copythink:

1. Know your customer.
2. Know your product.
3. Find the Central Selling Point.

But in the sales letter, you'll reverse the order of the first two steps. Since one of the reasons for selling by letter is that you can mail it to just the right customers, you must analyze your product first, to decide who will want and need it most.

Know Your Product

If you're writing a sales letter to glean new prospects or clients, your product will be your company's reputation for sound advice, good service, fast deliveries, and so forth. You should collect facts and figures, testimonials, and information about the company's history to shore up your claims and talk about them knowledgeably.

For example, if you're in the real estate business and want to find new clients, you can talk about "product" in terms of your sales record, citing the statistics that show how much property you've sold in the last year, where and what kind it is, and who your best-selling agents are. By analyzing your product, you'll be able to target the best customers for it. If, for example, you handle mainly business properties, you won't waste the letter by sending it to customers for one-family homes.

Nor will you try to sell baby carriages to bachelors or peanut brittle to denture wearers. Your product is the key to your target audience.

For example, let's assume that the local bank where you are head of customer service has decided to offer a new Home Equity Loan Program. You have been asked to write a sales letter introducing customers to this new service and explaining the tax advantages of home equity over regular consumer loans.

In order to decide who should get the letter, you must first understand the product:

It offers a number of advantages:

Tax-deductible interest no longer allowed under new tax laws for consumer loans.
Fast and easy application procedures, without red tape.
Approval within two weeks of application.
Loans in amounts up to 75 percent of home equity.
Convenient payment terms.
The lowest interest rates in town.
Loan money may be used to finance education, a car, home improvements, consumer purchases, or to consolidate credit card debt at a lower interest rate.

The bank has already test-marketed home equity loans, offering them during a trial period to selected customers, but you discovered that most of these people were wary of borrowing further on their homes, often their major financial investment. It's clear from this brief experience that customers will have some resistance to these loans, even with the promise of tax-deductible interest.

You decide that the best prospects for the new type of loan are homeowners who already have consumer loans, mortgages, or credit cards through your bank. They have good credit ratings, they've paid at a steady and on-time rate, they've been through the loan process before, and they are comfortably used to the tax deductions which, under the old tax law, helped pay for the loan. You could further screen your list by checking bank records for customers who use the bank's investment service or maintain large accounts for which any form of tax relief might be welcome.

If you can convince this group of customers that home equity loans make sense, you're sure that word-of-mouth advertising will do the rest. But you realize your toughest job will be to convince customers that it's okay to go the second mortgage route. You decide to focus your sales message on the benefits, not the negatives. You'll talk about how sensible it is to use a tax-deductible method to finance home improvements or a new car, how shrewd it is to tap into the safest investment of all, and how thrifty it is to borrow at these interest rates. You can also emphasize the pleasures of providing a college education for one's children, making room for the new baby, or enjoying more abundance in life.

With this overview in mind, use the who-what-when-where-how-and-why questions from the reader analysis checklist in Chapter One to focus on your customer. Anticipate the customer's questions about the loan and prepare answers. Prepare a One-Customer Profile to help you focus your sales letter:

> The customer for our new home equity loans is a new or established homeowner who already has a first mortgage, a consumer loan, or a credit card with the bank.
>
> This customer is most concerned about borrowing on a home, perhaps the family's biggest financial investment; is conservative in handling money, and welcomes new ways to save it; and is particularly interested in shielding it from the IRS.
>
> The customer is familiar with borrowing procedures, but may be wary of red tape and does not realize that a home equity loan is much simpler to process.

With your product and customer information at hand, you can decide on the best Central Selling Point, one which will demonstrate the benefits of your product for the customer. You decide that the money-saving benefits of the home equity loan will be the most appealing to your targeted customers: "The Smart Money: A Home Equity Loan from First National Can Save You a Bundle."

Now you're ready to write your sales letter, using the AIM format and emphasizing your Central Selling Point (see Figure 9–3).

Know Your Customer

Understanding your product helps you zero in on the right prospects for it. It's clear, for example, that the people most likely to buy your new fuel-saving pump for their furnace are homeowners, that the prospects for your mutual fund will be people with good incomes, and that the subscribers to your new magazine about the environment will be those already active in ecology groups and local environmental organizations.

You know that the customer for your new baby food will be the mother, not the baby. Babies have to eat it—and indicate their preferences in various clear ways—but they don't go out and buy it. You may also discover another market by analyzing your product. Baby food, for example, is also purchased by people who need a bland diet.

The demographics business. Everybody—from politicians to economists to Madison Avenue advertising agencies—would love to have X-ray vision into the consumer's head. They know that the key to sales is what's already going on in the minds of their customers.

In the absence of such X rays and crystal balls, some firms are doing

Figure 9–3.   A letter that sells a service.

THE SMART MONEY:
A HOME EQUITY LOAN FROM FIRST NATIONAL
CAN SAVE YOU A BUNDLE

December 7, 1986

Mr. Mortimer Snerd
73 Main Street
Peoria, IL 61601

Dear Mr. Snerd:

Have you heard the news?

Now you can make money the easy way, right in your own home.

As a homeowner, you're eligible for the best money-making break in town: a First National Home Equity Loan that will save you money on your income tax besides.

In a matter of two weeks from today, you could have the money for a new car or for college tuition sitting in your bank account, just by applying for a Home Equity Loan. And, although interest on other loans—for a car, a credit card, or a college degree—is no longer deductible under the new tax law, you can go ahead and deduct these interest payments from your income tax and help pay for the loan!

For a limited time, we're offering you and our other special customers a low interest rate of 7%, just because we want you to take advantage of this great tax-saving offer. We'll loan you up to 75% of the equity you've built up in your home, and give you a choice of convenient payment plans. Best of all, the application is simple— no red tape, no appraisers' fees, no mortgage tax—and we can let you know within two weeks from the time you apply if your loan is approved.

The smart money's headed for First National, Mr. Snerd, and we don't want you to miss out on this wonderful opportunity to save money on your taxes and finance your dreams. Take a look at the enclosed brochure. Then give me a call at 555-1234 or stop in at my office any day this week—I'll be waiting to hear from you!

Sincerely,

P. J. Morgan, Vice President
Customer Service

---

very well at analyzing and predicting what the consumer is going to do next. They're in the business of what's called demographics, or the study of populations. Basically, it's people research, to discern various marketing segments and discover the dynamics of buyer behavior at different age, education, and income levels. For example, a firm in California has produced a study of consumer thinking called "Values and Lifestyles" (VALS) that divides Americans into nine types according to their attitudes and the products they buy (see Figure 9–4).[1] Advertising agencies pay large yearly fees to subscribe to services like this.

Your own research and customer empathy are equally valuable in writing the sales letter. Using your knowledge of your product, decide on the best prospects for it. Then, run through the reader analysis checklist to help you get a picture of those customers. Formulate a One-Customer Profile to help you reach all customers with the appeals closest to their collective heart.

Some of the data in the VALS survey (see Figure 9–4) may help you understand the contemporary customer better. Some 1,635 people answered the VALS questionnaire, 85 pages of questions covering everything from sexual habits to brands of margarine to the kind of pets they owned. The results showed these values–and–life-styles groups:

1. *The Need-Driven* (11 percent of the population):
   Survivors (the elderly subsisting on Social Security, welfare recipients, anyone existing at subsistence level)
   Sustainers (gamblers, racetrack touts, others who survive on the fringes)

Figure 9–4.   The VALS double hierarchy of psychological maturity.

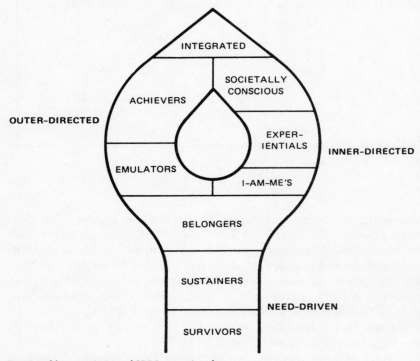

Reprinted by permission of SRI International.

2. *The Inner-Directed* (19 percent of the population):
   I-Am-Mes (rebellious youths, antiestablishment types)
   Experientials (those trying for the peak experience, the creative)
   Societally Conscious (political, social-issue-oriented people)
3. *The Outer-Directed* (68 percent of the population):
   Belongers (largest group—38 percent—traditional, conformist)
   Emulators (less conventional, trying to make it)
   Achievers (second largest group—20 percent—ambitious, driven, rich)
4. *The Integrated* (2 percent of the population):
   Both creative *and* prosperous.[2]

These VALS categories suggest one of many ways to think about your customer. Although most people are a blend of several of these categories, your understanding of your customer's values and life-style will help you echo these major concerns in your sales letters.

Mailing lists. Selling by mail depends heavily on audience analysis. A sales letter is successful only if it reaches the right customers.

Your company may already maintain its own lists of prospective clients that you can draw on for a mailing list. But you may need lists that target special audiences: lawyers, perhaps, or two-income families; parents of new babies; or first-time buyers of a luxury automobile, for example.

You can buy lists like these from firms that specialize in compiling mailing lists. Look in the Yellow Pages, or consult the *Guide to American Directories for Compiling Mailing Lists* at your local library. Or, you can write to the Direct Mail Advertising Association for help.

Before you pay for a mailing list, be sure to check on how it was compiled and how up to date it is.

Find the Central Selling Point

Once you've analyzed your product and your customer, the next step in planning the sales letter is to find the Central Selling Point. Pick the main feature of your product, the one that distinguishes it from others. Then check over your audience analysis. What does your customer need or want that your product will satisfy?

Match the ease and convenience of the express banking service to the customer's desire for fast service. Match the pure, natural flavor of the baby food to the mother's concern about nutrition. Match the exclusivity of the high-priced burglar alarm to the customer's need to be special—and secure.

The Central Selling Point focuses the sales message on the main feature of the product as it translates into a benefit for the customer. If you're offering the same product to different groups of customers, the Central Selling Point may change.

For example, a new minivan may appeal to people who need to carry lots of items around or who have large families. For these customers, play up the van's load and seating capacity.

To attract a sports car enthusiast, you'd have to emphasize the van's good looks, performance, and streamlining. And to sell it to people who like pickup trucks, you should talk durability, strength, and front-wheel drive.

Deciding on the Central Selling Point means tailoring your product's appeal to your target audience. It's a decision that gives the sales letter its strategic approach.

The Structure of the Sales Letter

To sell at maximum, the sales letter must be organized in successive stages of appeal. The AIM format is designed to simulate the process of selling—and buying:

Attention: Get the customer to listen.
Interest: Arouse the customer's desire.
Motivation: Convince the customer.
Call to action: Urge the sale.

These are the basic stages of the sales process, in person or on paper.

In person, you'd know how much time to devote to each step, since you would be getting feedback from the customer and could watch his reactions. On paper, you need to cover the steps in the right order and in sufficient detail so that it's all there in writing if the customer wishes to reread and consider your proposition.

Get Attention

Most of the special tactics already discussed have as their purpose getting attention in the sales letter. It's the primary task of the letter's first paragraph. Here are some good ways to do it.

Talk about the reader. The basic attention-getting method in persuasion is to connect with the reader's own experience or mind-set as soon as possible. That's the purpose of using personal names and addresses. It doesn't hurt to use the customer's name in the first paragraph, or to repeat it a few times throughout the letter.

Talk about the reader in the first paragraph:

As one of our best customers, Mrs. Smith, you're . . .
The car you just purchased at Motown Motors is the finest money can buy.
Every Christmas, you've got the same problem: what to give the person who has everything.
You've just moved to Brownsville, and we'd like to welcome you to town.

Tell a story. Stories and anecdotes have always been a salesperson's stock-in-trade; they get customers involved. But the story must be connected to your product or sales message to be effective in persuasion.

Don't start out talking about football and switch to selling aluminum siding unless the connection's clear.

Here are some examples of sentences to start a story:

> There are a lot of people who wish they'd heard about the XYZ plan *last* year.
> Let me tell you about. . .

Here are some ways to use narrative in the first paragraph:

> When you were growing up, a dollar bill would go a long way. You could blow it all at the candy store and get enough sweets to be sick for a week. Or you could go to the Saturday afternoon double feature and have change for popcorn. *(Brokerage firm letter)*
>
> John and Jane Doe decided to sell their home themselves when they were getting ready to move. They figured they'd save the commission and come out ahead in the long run.
>
> They put up a big sign out front, advertised in the paper, and sat back to await the flood of buyers who'd soon be knocking on the door.
>
> Six months later, they're still waiting. *(Real estate agent's letter)*

The sales letter in Figure 9–5 attracts attention by talking about the reader and beginning to tell a story, effectively picturing for her what it would be like to own the product the letter has been written to sell. The letter, constructed according to the AIM format, builds interest by talking about benefits of ownership. A motivation section, beginning with the last paragraph on the first page, describes facts about the product and moves into an offer ("no obligation to purchase") and a Call to Action, with an attention-getting postscript to highlight a special benefit of purchase.

Ask a question. Questions at the beginning of a sales letter set up an automatic reaction in readers, who feel compelled to answer or to read on to find the answer. Again, the question must be connected to the sales message and the product. Here are some examples:

> What's the one thing you should know about buying a computer?
> If you could take your pick, where would you *really* like to spend your vacation this year?
> Just once, wouldn't you like to get lucky on the stock market?

(continued on p. 150)

Figure 9–5.   A sample sales letter.

Dear Cardmember:

Imagine that one of your ancestors, generations ago, had acquired a flatware service of solid sterling silver and had passed it on to you. Think how fortunate you would feel.

Aside from its value, that family silver would give you very special feelings of pride and satisfaction. Every time you set your table with it, you would enjoy its weight. Its generous proportions. Its fine workmanship. Its unmistakable quality.

> Now, as an American Express Cardmember, you have the exclusive opportunity to acquire your own family silver of the same high quality—a silver service whose weight and beauty and size and workmanship rival those services of old.

It is crafted of <u>solid sterling silver</u> embellished with <u>pure 24 carat extra heavy gold electroplate</u>. Its design is classic . . . elegant . . . beautiful. Crafted in the large European size, it has excellent weight—not just by today's standards but by the standards of generations past. Its workmanship is extraordinarily intricate, delicate, and refined. It is, in every respect, a service of superlative quality.

By special arrangement, this magnificent gold and silver service is now being offered <u>exclusively to American Express Cardmembers</u>. It is not available through any other sources—not even the finest jewellers or museums. Your service will be crafted expressly for you by the skilled artisans of Gorham—the modern inheritors of Gorham's 151-year tradition of excellence. Each piece will be finished for you, by hand, in the old-fashioned way. In fact, no fewer than 143 hand operations are involved in each four-piece place setting of Golden Dunstan.

> In the tradition of family silver, each piece will bear your family initial, hand engraved through the gold in an elegant script. What's more, each piece of your Golden Dunstan service will be engraved for you with your own personal registration number. This registration number will be recorded and kept by Gorham in

perpetuity. And whenever you or your heirs add to your service, each additional piece will be engraved by Gorham with the same number.

This exclusive opportunity to acquire the Golden Dunstan service of gold and silver flatware—classic in design, generous in weight, and an important family heirloom of the future—is one you should consider carefully. During the past decade, the price of silver has risen more than six times over what it used to be. And this has, of course, had its effect on the prices of silver products. But through this exclusive invitation, you can acquire your complete service of Golden Dunstan flatware and take advantage of our convenient monthly payment plan at no additional charge.

The enclosed brochure illustrates and describes this magnificent silverware. But there is no substitute for actually seeing it close up and as part of your own table settings. Holding each piece in your hand. Feeling its weight and its perfect balance.

We therefore cordially invite you to examine your Golden Dunstan service in your own home for 15 days <u>with no obligation to purchase</u>. When you do, I am sure you will be convinced that this is one of the most rewarding and worthwhile acquisitions you could possibly make. For your own enjoyment from day to day. For entertaining—whether an informal buffet or the most formal dining occasion. And to pass on as a legacy of enduring beauty to future generations of your family.

Sincerely,

Robert L. Meyers
Senior Vice President

P.S.   This exclusive offer from American Express makes it possible for you to realize substantial savings when you order your Golden Dunstan Silver in sets. By ordering service for four or eight, the cost of each place setting is significantly reduced. See the enclosed Reservation Form for complete details.

Reprinted by permission of American Express.

Ever wonder how your neighbors manage to keep their lawns looking so good?

One word of caution: Be sure the question you ask can't be answered no!

Split a sentence. The simple device of splitting a sentence can lead
readers into the sales letter. Like the series of one-sentence paragraphs,
the split sentence compels the reader to read on; the elliptical statements
leave something to the imagination:

> For all you do . . .
>   this Bud's for you.   *(Budweiser)*
> Babies are our business . . .
>   and have been for 50 years.   *(Gerber)*
> If you need more than Bayer Aspirin . . .
>   see your doctor.   *(Bayer)*

Tell the news. Announce the news at the beginning of a sales letter
for attention-getting effect:

> Our 50 percent OFF SALE starts as soon as you get this letter.
> More Americans will travel to Europe this summer than at any time
>   in our history.
> We've just cut the cost of going to college!

Cite a quotation. Pertinent words from famous people or testimonials from satisfied customers or celebrities can provide attention-getting
openers for the sales letter:

> In the future, everyone will be world-famous for fifteen min-
> utes.
>
> —Andy Warhol

> Life is painting a picture, not doing a sum.
>
> —Oliver Wendell Holmes

> "There isn't a better battery on the market for the money,"
> says one satisfied customer.

Indulge in word play. Readers can be attracted by your cleverness if
it's not too farfetched. Puns and double entendres can be effective come-

ons in the sales letter because they offer new ways to think about a product:

> Bake someone happy. *(Betty Crocker)*
> Fall. Catch it before it leaves. *(New England Tourist Board)*
> We'll make you an overnight success. *(Express Mail)*

Attention-getters can be as outrageous and clever as you like, as long
as they're keyed to the product you're selling and to your audience. But
like jokes, puns can be misunderstood. Anything that might leave potential buyers saying "Huh?" or merely admiring your clever words won't
tempt them to read on or buy.

Build Interest

Once the customer is reading, the sales letter must move on to build
interest in the product. Describe it in vivid, concrete language. Fit it to
your reader's needs (see Figure 9–6). Talk benefits. Use the Central Selling Point and dramatize the product as if it were already part of the
customer's life. Sell use:

> In your own seaside villa, you can put your feet up and sip Papaya
> Punch while you watch the sun do gown over azure waters.

> With DentaFoam, brushing your teeth will be a whole new experi-
> ence. Your mouth will feel cleaner because it is. And your teeth will
> *look* cleaner because DentaFoam's foaming action gets where ordi-
> nary toothpaste can't.

> You'll save money on long-distance calls right from the beginning
> with Phonomatic because there's no installation fee. And with our
> Prime Rates, you can pick your own time to make your calls.

People do like to read, in great detail, about what they'll get if they
buy your product. Spare nothing in describing how the customer will
feel, look, and live when using it (as long as your claims are authentic);
talk benefits and sell use.

Don't make the mistake of describing only product features. Always
link them to a benefit for the reader.

Play up the positive. People respond to and remember positives better than negatives. If you want them to *say* yes, you must *talk* yes.

A negative Central Selling Point, for example, gives your message

Figure 9–6. Echo the reader and fit the message to the reader's needs.

You've been asked to write sales letters introducing your company's new Bionic® rubber fabric that, like a second skin, lets air in but keeps rain out, stretches for comfort but keeps its shape, can be dyed any color, and has a smooth and attractive surface. The fabric can be used in hospital dressings, space suits, rain gear, sports equipment, even car seats.

Solution: Draft different versions of the same letter to reach different readers. Your analysis shows the best way to echo each reader and fit the message to that reader's needs:

Doctors	Concerned with treating surgical wounds, dressings, healing; need barrier to bacteria *and* aeration of wound, comfort to patient
Space scientists	Care about weight, scientific properties of fabric, protection, breathability, comfort to wearer
Rain gear manufacturers	Want protection from weather that solves problem of air circulation; cost a concern
Sports equipment manufacturers	Need fabric that will be comfortable during strenuous exercise, easily shaped, stretchable, breathable; cost a concern
Automobile companies	Care about appearance, wear, and comfort; cost a concern
Women's clothing manufacturers	Appearance, fit, drapability, color; cost a concern

---

negative connotations in the reader's mind. Rephrase it, say, from *Don't catch another cold this winter* to *Be healthy all winter.*

Provide Motivation

The third paragraph or section of the sales letter must convince customers that your product is everything you've said. Facts, figures, testimonials, guarantees, and warranty information here will give readers the proof they need to make up their minds. This is also a good place to mention price, since it will be surrounded by factual information and solid proof of value.

> Studies show that nine out of 10 people need some kind of health care in every 12-month period. Our XYZ health plan cuts the cost of doctor visits by half and pays *all* prescription drug bills—but you'll pay just pennies a week for these healthy savings.

We've been in the used-car business for 50 years, right on Main Street. My grandfather started out on the same corner in 1937, and he offered a money-back guarantee with every automobile he sold. We're still making that guarantee.

You must mention price somewhere in the sales letter, since it's usually one of the customer's first questions and can be an important selling point. But always mention it in terms of a benefit:

The Always Alert smoke alarm comes complete with battery for just $19.99, a small price to pay for 24-hour protection.

Or give a ballpark figure that offers the customer a sense of the savings:

You'll get up-to-the-minute stock analysis for less than $5.50 a week. That's less than it would cost you in gas to go down to the broker's office and watch the ticker.

Put price in a long sentence, as here, or talk about it in small units, as monthly amounts or a down payment.

You can hold off revealing price if you want to induce the customer to follow up: *"Just send the handy enclosed postcard back for more details on this special offer."* But you run the risk that, without the price, the customer won't care enough to do this.

Make your offer here. Now's the time, after you've built motivation for purchase, to introduce your offer. Everything you've said to this point has been leading up to making the sale. The offer helps you by giving the reader an extra inducement to act, just before you make your call to action.

Call to Action

The end is always the best place to suggest purchase in a sales letter. It's the last part the reader sees, and the one she's likely to remember best.

Make action simple, easy, and urgent. A reply postcard, a toll-free telephone number, or an appointment for a salesperson's visit will lower the reader's sense of risk as she ponders the decision to buy.

Add a sense of urgency: set a deadline, and offer a benefit for complying:

If you order before December 15, we'll send you a free personal address book in the color of your choice.

Always remind the customer of benefits as you ask for action:

You'll start saving money the day you receive your new Express-Check card. Don't wait any longer to make banking a breeze.

Use the postscript to sell. A postscript after your signature attracts attention to a special point you'd like to emphasize or repeat:

P.S. Our budget plan makes VideoRock easy to own. Just indicate the payment plan you prefer on the enclosed postcard.

Testing Your Sales Letter

One of the advantages of selling by mail is that you can get an accurate measure of results. Every sale you make comes from a customer who received your letter.

However, professionals in direct-mail selling estimate that a good rate of return is just between 3 and 5 percent of your total mailing. If you mail out 1,000 letters, in other words, you can reasonably expect to hear from about 30 customers.

At this rate, advertisers who sell by mail on a regular basis like to test their copy and sales approach on a small scale first, to make sure it's on target with the customer. They choose a small segment of the mailing list, and send out a shorter version of the planned mailing piece, perhaps using just the basic concept in a headline and the offer.

The results give them more assurance about the sales approach, or suggest that a change is in order. If, after a first effort with your sales letter, you decide to change it, be careful. Don't change the whole thing; revise only one aspect of the message at a time—the headline, the offer, or perhaps the Central Selling Point. Otherwise, there will be no way to tell what the winning combination is.

Tone in the Sales Letter

The attitude you convey in the sales letter—your tone—is crucial to its success. You need to sound confident without bragging, and you want to generate enthusiasm without overdoing it. Above all, you want to sound trustworthy and believable.

As long as you stick to the facts about your product, service, or idea, you'll come off with a good credibility rating. An informative, factual approach conveys sincerity to the reader. Good customer empathy also saves you from overstating your case.

Tone is a matter of language. Good solid nouns and verbs sell more believably than crescendos of adjectives and adverbs. Instead of *This fantastic, incredibly brilliant necklace is a real sparkler,* use nouns and verbs to sell: *This zircon necklace sparkles like real diamonds that would cost 10 times as much.*

As in all persuasive writing, be positive. It puts the reader in the right mood and gives your letter an inevitable enthusiasm.

Check with the Post Office

Unless you've hired another firm to do the actual mailing for you, it would be wise to check postal regulations and rates for bulk mail as you plan your sales letter. You'll keep costs down by designing it to conform to post office standards.

For example, there are rules about the size of envelopes for mailing, and the post office charges more for overweight or oversize envelopes. Find out about bulk mail rates and quantities, and arrange for a permit number for your postage-paid reply cards.

Chapter Ten
Writing Your Own Ads

You can use the valuable lessons you've already learned about persuasion in this book to write your own advertisements. Indeed, many of these lessons were tested first in the world of advertising, where persuasive techniques have been developed and used particularly well for many years.

Perhaps you run a small business you'd like to promote with circulars or newspaper display ads. Or you've developed a growing mail-order clientele, and you'd like to write some catalog copy that will sell.

Maybe you're a beginning copywriter who'd like some tips on how to do your job better. Managers and entrepreneurs who understand copywriting can work with advertising agencies more effectively.

Use Special Tactics

Persuasive techniques in advertising differ from those in a letter or memo in special ways:

- Advertising sells visually.
- Advertising simplifies the selling message to get it across fast.
- Advertising sells on its headline. Body copy and artwork must be keyed to it.

Think Visually

A good print advertisement is designed for the eye. It's competing with all those other ads for the customer's attention, and it needs an eye-catching picture, layout, or headline—preferably all three—to arrest the glance of the skimming reader. An ad must get the message across visually first, before its words have a chance to take effect.

You must think in both words and pictures as you plan a selling strategy for an ad. Even though your artistic ability may be limited to drawing stick figures, you can learn to visualize and sketch out your ideas well enough to plot a total selling concept for an advertisement. There are basic visual patterns, for example, that you can use to draft a "rough" of your ideas, enough to show an art department what you have in mind. (See figure 10–1.)

You can also get expert advice about layout and artwork when you're planning an ad yourself. For example, most newspaper advertising departments can help with design suggestions and offer what's called "clip art," ready-made illustrations you can choose from.

A local graphic arts firm might do layouts for you on the basis of your ideas. And you can study print ads yourself to pick up tips on what works best visually.

Eventually, you'll want professional help to prepare the final ad for publication. But here are some guidelines to help you think visually about it:

1. *Plan to allow for some or all of these basic elements in the layout:*

   Headline
   Illustrations/photos and captions
   Body copy
   Subheadings
   Price
   Company logo, name, and address

2. *Design a layout that's easy for the eye to follow:*

   - Think in terms of the reader's eye movement, from left to right.
   - Remember that the focal point of an ad is above and to the left of center, at "10 o'clock." Place headlines or a picture here to arrest the eye.
   - Follow the clockwise (left-to-right) movement of the eye as you add other elements to the layout. If you've used a picture at 10

o'clock, keep up the momentum with a headline at the right, at 2 o'clock.
- Plan the layout so that it isn't lopsided. It doesn't have to be perfectly balanced; in fact, assymmetry is more interesting to the eye. But make sure that everything isn't lumped all on one side or at the top.

Figure 10–1. Basic visual patterns for an advertising layout.

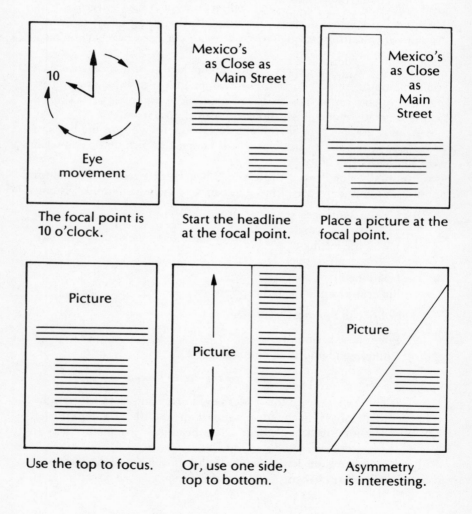

The focal point is 10 o'clock.

Start the headline at the focal point.

Place a picture at the focal point.

Use the top to focus.

Or, use one side, top to bottom.

Asymmetry is interesting.

- Use white space to frame and balance your written message. Generous margins focus the eye. An ad that's too crowded tends to run together.

    Some advertisers use white space to give the image of luxury to their product, selling it with just a picture and a headline, and no copy. Crowded ads, sometimes used by supermarkets and retailers, project another image: discount, bargain, variety.
- Be bold: use one large headline and one large picture for more impact than a dozen smaller ones.
- For extra eye appeal, use color.
- Use a border all around the edges of your ad to set it off.

3. *Choose artwork to focus the ad on one of the following:*

- The product itself
- The Central Selling Point
- Your company image

For authenticity, use photographs. To set a mood or create an image, use artist's illustrations.

4. *Make body copy easy to read:*

- Less is more. Keep the copy block in proportion to other elements. If you have to choose, make pictures big, copy short.
- Keep sentences short: seven to 11 words for easiest reading. Use single words and fragmented sentences to give your sales talk the feeling of conversation.
- Paragraph frequently.
- Use familiar, concrete words.

Simplify the Selling Concept

A well-focused, simplified selling concept will give your advertisement instant appeal and invite a reading. Stick to One Big Idea, carried out in the headline, the artwork, and the body copy. Usually, that big idea will be the Central Selling Point of your product or service.

Know Your Product

With ads as with sales letters, your Copythink planning should begin with a thorough review of your product. It's the key to your target audience. And you do want to sound as if you know what you're talking about.

If you're selling hand-dipped chocolates, for example, get to know every step in the process, all about the ingredients, and the whole story on packaging and delivery. Pass out samples and get people's reactions.

If it's a new appliance you're promoting, try it out yourself. Watch customers on the selling floor as they examine the appliance, and ask them questions. Read the spec sheets and find out about service contracts and warranties.

Maybe you've just opened a restaurant and want to advertise. Go over your menu, the decor you've arranged, the lighting, seating, and price range to look for special selling points.

With information at hand, you're ready to focus on the customer. Figure out who has to buy your product, who needs it but doesn't know about it, and who might buy if you make it appealing enough.

Know Your Customer

When it comes to chocolates, your potential market is probably a big one, already out there and waiting. Except for dieters and those with health problems, most people like candy, especially chocolate. And it's an accepted gift at birthdays, holidays, and other special occasions.

Your hand-dipped chocolates, individually wrapped in gold paper and boxed in attractive Art Deco containers, have a slightly narrower appeal, however. The customers for these are probably people looking for a gift item or the connoisseurs who will buy only special candy.

Probably your target audience will be those looking for something out of the ordinary. You'll aim to attract the gourmet, gift-giving segment of the market, not the chocolate-bar-for-the-movies crowd.

Depending on its location and cuisine, the restaurant you've opened can have a potential townwide range of customers. But let's say that yours is the first Tex-Mex place in town and that your prices are à la carte.

Your customers may be among the cognoscenti who are willing to pay for being in the know about good food. Others, like the people who want to say they've been there whether they like enchiladas or not and the couple going out for a special night, will also be likely to stop in at least once.

Your market will not be the hordes of college students in town who keep the local beanery in business. It will probably be an upscale group who, if they like the restaurant, will help it become one of the "in" spots.

The customers for your product or service are already out there; it's up to you and your ingenuity to focus on their special needs.

Write to Just One Customer

Compose a One-Customer Profile for your advertisement. The Tex-Mex restaurant ad, for example, could focus on a customer who would like to consider himself ahead of the crowd, someone who is or who fancies himself to be something of a cosmopolite, and whose interest in food has gone way beyond mere hunger. Your appeal to your customer's sophisticated tastes—or desire for them—will draw in *all* the customers who think of themselves in this way.

There's always a large group of customers who aren't specifically "in the market." But you can make customers out of them. A strong Central Selling Point that gives them a reason to buy will add them to your clientele.

Find the Central Selling Point

What's the strongest feature of your product? What distinguishes it from others of the same kind? And, what benefits does it offer the customer you have in mind?

The individually wrapped, hand-dipped chocolates, packed in fancy gift boxes, offer their specialness in a world full of candy. They say "one-of-a-kind" to all the customers who would like to be special or to make someone else feel that way.

As your Central Selling Point, you might play up the preparation and packaging of the chocolates to the customer who wants "unique" as much as she wants chocolates. The care and attention that go into them translate as emotional benefits to this customer.

The Tex-Mex restaurant in the center of town won't have to lure its customers from afar. The best Central Selling Point for both product feature and customer benefit is the food, as something new in town with potential for status ("*Where can you find a decent enchilada in Cleveland?*" or, maybe, "*What's an enchilada?*").

Your choice of a Central Selling Point is crùcial because the entire ad, from headline to art to copy, will be focused on this One Big Idea.

Make the Headline Work

The common wisdom is that a good headline is worth 80 percent of the advertising dollar. It's true: *an ad sells on its headline.* Next to the artwork, the first thing a reader will notice in an ad is the headline. It should interest him enough to make him want to read the copy. It must also sell, and be totally tuned in to the ad's concept and art.

Every word in a headline must work for its living. Although there's no particular restriction on length, the demands of space and a pica count usually mean that a headline must work on a few well-chosen words.

There are certain words that always work in headlines, as David Ogilvy has noted. Some of them are "new," "free," "now," "announcing," "introducing," "quick," "easy," and "last chance." Emotional words like "love," "baby," "friend," and "darling" pull readership, too, he says.[1]

Write the Headline First

The headline sets up the strategy for the rest of the ad and provides a focal point to work with as you write the copy. Write it first.

Draw on your experience in writing "grabbers" for sales letters. Use the Central Selling Point. Or design headlines around one of these proven attention-getters:

- *Use the you-approach:*

  Your new Ultra-Vision set is waiting for you right now at Baltman's.
  Move into the 21st Century today, with Ultra-Vision.
  Ultra-Vision puts you in the 21st Century.

- *Make a promise:*

  Chocolate that says she's your one-and-only.
  Give her a sample of your good taste.

- *Ask a question:*

  How come they didn't think of this when you were a kid?!
  Don't you wish they made all kids' clothes with Velcro®?

- *Arouse curiosity with a "teaser":*

  Enchilada tonight in Peoria
  Some people come here just for our swizzle sticks.

- *Tell the news (sometimes the best news is price):*

  Now you can book Bermuda on your lunch hour.
  We've cut the red tape in travel.
  Announcing the $99 trip to the sun

- *Use word play:*

  Sweet-talk her with Minerva Chocolates.
  Mexico's as close as Main Street.
  Warm up with a bowl of our chili.

- *Tell a story:*

  How one New Jersey couple fell in love all over again
  When he showed up with the Minerva Chocolates, she knew it
  was time to forgive and forget.

- *Use a quotation:*

  "But, darling, wait 'til you see the pink sand in Eleuthera."
  "We don't eat out much, but when we do, it's always Pedro's."

Remember that a headline doesn't have to be a complete sentence. The picture you use with it can supply some of its meaning. The headline doesn't always have to contain the product name, but it must be relevant to the copy that follows or the reader will be confused.

Study some of the following slogans and headlines for ideas about how to attract attention and use the Central Selling Point. Some of them have been so successful that they've become part of the language:

You're going to like us. *(TWA)*
You got it. *(Toyota)*
We're your type. *(IBM)*
Coke is it. *(Coca-Cola)*
Thomas' promises. *(Thomas' English Muffins)*
We've been working on the railroad. *(Amtrak)*
Come to where the flavor is. *(Marlboro)*
You've come a long way, baby. *(Virginia Slims)*
Where's the beef? *(Wendy's)*
Does she or doesn't she? *(Clairol)*

Key Copy to the Headlines

Think of copy as a short composition, with the headline as its thesis. Or consider the headline as your first paragraph and write everything else to support it. An ad sells on relevant, well-worded copy.

Use AIM. Make a quick outline of points, using the AIM format. Streamline your copy to attention, interest, and motivation sections.

A stands for *attention*. The first paragraph should pick up where the headline left off, to get attention and keep readers involved. Here's how an ad for the chocolates might move from headline to first paragraph:

Sweet-talk her with MINERVA CHOCOLATES

You-approach	When you want to tell her she's special, there's nothing that says it better than a one-of-a-kind box of our hand-dipped chocolates. Let Minerva do your sweet-talking for you.

Other examples:

News:	Ultra-Vision puts you in the 21st Century, right now
	Step into the future today at Baltman's and take a look at technology that'll put you and your family into a 21st Century of television viewing.
Story:	How come they didn't think of this when you were a kid?
	Remember all the struggles you had when you were learning to dress yourself, with buttons that wouldn't button, and zippers that always seemed to get stuck? Sometimes it seemed like you'd never learn. And now that you have children of your own, you still wish somebody would make dressing a two-year-old simpler.
Curiosity:	Some people come here just for our swizzle sticks
	They're starting to collect those little green swizzlers with the gold parrot that we put in every Margarita we serve at Pedro's.
	But if that's all you came for, you'd be missing a whole world of exotic things, all waiting for you on our menu.
Curiosity and story:	Now you can book Bermuda on your lunch hour
	Used to be, when you were planning a trip, you had to plan the trip to the travel agent, too, allowing plenty of time for the inevitable wait and red tape.
	No more, not at. . . .

I stands for *interest*. In the interest section of your copy, you must match product facts with customer benefits—the Central Selling Point. For example:

Every piece of our candy is lovingly dipped, by hand, in chocolate so rich she'll wonder if it's legal. At the center, she'll find all kinds of surprises—fresh almonds, creamy mints, velvety caramels, and orange-flavored liqueurs. All wrapped, one at a time, in thick gold paper.

Sample our nachos with fresh avocado and pepper cheese, or order up our Texas-size appetizer platter brimming with south-of-the-border selections. Let our caballeros serenade you while you decide between the gazpacho and the guacamole.

M stands for *motivation*. To involve the customer enough to motivate a purchase, remember to offer solid facts that give your claims credibility in the third segment of the ad. The customer who has read this far is already interested. Your motivation section now provides the information that "proves" your selling point.

Because we import our own cocoa beans and get our cream and fresh butter from local dairies, we can afford to make chocolate that's probably the richest you've ever tasted. The recipe's a secret, but we can tell you it's been in the family for three generations, and nobody else has been able to duplicate it—though they've tried.

The *call to action*. Save the last sentence or paragraph of copy to suggest action. Combine it with a reminder of benefits:

If your love life's been a little sour lately, try some sweet talk from Minerva. Pick up a box on your way home tonight.

She'll get the message.

Observe Copy Dos and Don'ts

In advertising copy as in persuasive letters and memos, it's the connection you make between product feature and customer benefit—the Central Selling Point—that makes a sale. What's in it for me? is always the customer's first question. Your copy should focus on answering it.

Rhetorical raptures about the product are just so many words until you *dramatize* it as part of the customer's own life. She's looking for a sample-in-print. As you write, remember these points:

Dramatize: sell use. Describe the product in action so that the customer can imagine it in his own life:

Your first bite of a Minerva chocolate will tell you how special it is.

Use concrete, sensuous language. As in poetry, it's picture-making language that makes your product real to a reader. Use concrete nouns and verbs; take it easy on the adjectives. And remember that a factual, understated message is more believable:

Playclothes in the kind of crayon colors kids can really get into
How to turn a business trip into a pleasure jaunt
Chili you could eat with a fork
Chocolate that's like a kiss from someone you love
Once you thought this kind of technology existed only in Buck Rogers

Write as if you were talking to the reader. Use natural, familiar language. In fact, the more conversational your copy sounds, the better its chances of connecting with the reader.

Direct address—using "you"—works especially well in advertising to involve potential customers. And contractions, sentence fragments, and even one-word "sentences" will give copy the flavor of conversation.

A more formal language, written in the third person, can create a special mood or image, too, depending on what you're selling. But be careful not to eliminate anybody by sounding too haughty.

Use short words, short sentences, and short paragraphs. You have a lot of competition in advertising, where you fight the same battle against reader resistance that you do in other written persuasion.

It pays to make your copy look easy to read. This is best accomplished with frequent paragraphs, sentences in the 17- to 22-word range, and words most people are familiar with. Depending on your audience, you may need to use technical words or special phrasing to describe a product. But tailor your vocabulary to reach your target audience.

The mass audience is better educated these days, but most people still like to take their information in the easiest way possible.

Be positive. People tend to remember the good things and forget the bad. Don't suggest negatives or build your case on them. Offer solutions, not problems.

Meet the Catalog Challenge

Writing product descriptions for catalogs is a special challenge. The customer can't run out to a store and try on the dress or see for herself if the tureen's big enough to serve soup to eight people. Your copy has to tell her everything she needs to know—and sell it to her—on its own.

Usually, you'll have to accomplish this in just one paragraph, with room for a short headline and a price. Add product colors, sizes, and fabric content or specifications, and that doesn't leave much room to talk benefits or create a mood.

Catalog pictures will do much of the selling for you. But your copy has to do its selling in just a few words because of space limitations. You may have just the headline and the beginning of a sentence to create a "buy me" situation. Factual, understated copy describing the product will do the rest.

For example, copy that sells the soup tureen might set the tone by selling use:

> *THE PARTY TUREEN:* Serve up lobster bisque at your next dinner party in a handsome, creamy white tureen. Complete with lid, ladle, and platter in softly glazed earthenware with scroll design. By Ceramics East. $49.95

Here, one word—"party"—takes the tureen out of the ordinary into an elegant dinner setting.

Mail-order catalogs like those put out by department stores sometimes have an overall theme to support the copy, or a running narrative that gives unity to the entire catalog. To suggest your company's service attitude, you could also include tips, recipes, or quotations along with product information. This is an excellent way to sell use.

Choose Your Ad Medium

In advertising agencies, whole departments of media planners do nothing but plot, analyze, and test the success of various media for ads. They know which newspaper or magazine or broadcast station has the right audience for a particular product, which times and seasons bring in the most response, and which pages in a woman's magazine or hours on a talk station pull the most customers.

Your own research can get you some of this high-powered information, too. At the very least, it will help you place your ads where your best customers are bound to see or hear about it.

The medium you choose for your ad will also determine, in some measure, how you plan and write your ad.

Newspapers. Published on a daily basis and covering a specific territory, newspapers are an excellent and timely medium for reaching local customers. Newspaper readers tend to be adults, however, rather than the young, who haven't yet acquired the same newspaper-reading habits.

Check circulation figures and delivery areas beforehand to be sure you'll cover your target market. Remember that a morning paper will reach a business audience better than an afternoon edition, which has more home and family coverage.

Discuss your advertising needs with the newspaper's own ad department to get tips on placement and timing for best exposure. You might want to put your restaurant ad in the business section to attract a lunch crowd, for example. Or the ad for children's clothes in the Living section, near the pediatrician's daily advice column. And many people think that the best place for a display ad is the right-hand page, next to reading matter.

Timing's important, too. Holidays, paydays, and school vacations in your local area are worth consideration when you place your ad. The best time to sell chocolates, for example, is probably Valentine's Day. Consider an ad or a special insert in the Sunday paper, since people typically take more time to read on the weekend.

Space is sold on the basis of columns and inches. You should check newspaper rates for display and classified ads to choose the space that fits your budget—and your message.

Disadvantages: Your ad will have a short life, and probably won't have the pass-along possibilities a magazine can give you. Newsprint doesn't reproduce some kinds of artwork as well as glossier paper does. And young people don't read newspapers the way their parents do.

Magazines. Magazines are a good place to reach a very specific group of customers. They're usually already well aimed at one particular segment of the market—men, women, sports enthusiasts, gourmets, teenagers. And readers tend to be consumers. Reproduction of artwork is generally better. And your copy can be longer.

Ask to see the magazine's reader profile, circulation figures, and territories. Review editorial content to consider how your message will fit in.

It's generally more expensive to advertise in magazines, but they do have pass-along readership beyond their circulation figures, and your ad will be around longer than in a newspaper. Someone sitting in a dentist's office could come across it a month later and become a customer.

Again, ask for advice from the magazine's advertising staff on placement and timing for your ad. Find out about special holiday issues and rates.

Prime spots: Inside the front cover, the back cover, near the front, and in the middle of the magazine.

Disadvantages: You might want to reach a wider audience than the magazine can deliver. For the money, you might get more mileage in its special regional editions.

Radio. Locally, this is a relatively inexpensive way to reach a specific audience. Most stations have listener profiles, and you may already know which station will appeal to your particular customers.

Timing is important. Choose rush-hour scheduling to reach commuters in their cars; daytime for an at-home market or for after school; evenings and weekends for a broader audience.

Copy for a radio advertisement is written for the ear, not the eye. It must use words with instant recognition and short, easy-to-listen-to sentences. Although the persuasive tactics presented in this book are designed for print, the same simple, focused strategy will sell on the air, too. But ask for some expert advice, and remember that you'll have only between 10 and 60 seconds to get the message across.

Disadvantages: Listeners can't go back and read what you've said if they missed something (repetition in a radio ad is important), and the potential distractions are many.

Television. Television commercials are expensive, but they probably cover the market better than any other medium, particularly to get a product image across. More than 85 percent of American households now have television sets.

Television offers the most complete medium for selling, appealing to both the eye and the ear. Advertising messages are plotted on storyboards to show picture-and-text sequence. Simple messages with big visual impact work best.

Timing and program ratings are of primary importance in considering placement for your ad. You'll need expert advice and professional help to put together the best advertising package for a television audience.

Disadvantages: Television advertising is expensive and competition for attention is fierce.

Or you can reach the buying public as they commute to work, check out their purchases at the cash register, or retrieve their mail from their mailboxes:

Car cards. Advertising on buses or subways, or even on shopping carts, gives you a "captive" audience. Your message has a good chance of being read and understood. But it should be simple, timely, visually interesting, and large enough to be seen from a seat.

Point-of-purchase placards. Advertising placards placed right on the counter remind customers of products and special purchases. These should be simple and easy to read from several angles. Bold headlines, prices, and purchase information will usually be enough.

Circulars. A tabloid-size circular you can distribute to homes or pass out at the store should be as well focused as an ad you publish. You can use circulars to publicize one-time sales or to reach very specific customers. Like sales letters, they go right to the home. An arresting headline is especially important.

The Challenge of Advertising

Some of the best user-friendly writing is done in the service of advertising. It's not quite fair that advertising has been viewed negatively by the general public, since it represents communication techniques at their most successful. It can teach us a great deal about effective sales tactics.

Once you get the hang of it, writing copy for your own advertisements or persuasive letters can bring out your best. The range of imaginative possibilities, coupled with the discipline of getting the sales message across, offers a writing exercise that demands skill and talent in using the language.

Persuasion can be manipulative and become propaganda at the turn of a phrase. But the best advertising is designed to take the interests of the customer to heart. It makes good writers into better ones as it teaches one basic lesson: your writing is as persuasive as your sense of the reader. That one lesson can make persuasive writers of us all.

For Further Reading

On Writing and Language

Flesch, Rudolf. *The ABC of Style: A Guide to Plain English*. New York: Harper & Row, 1965.

Hayakawa, S. I. *Language in Thought and Action,* 3rd ed. New York: Harcourt Brace Jovanovich, 1972.

Roman, Kenneth, and Joel Raphaelson. *Writing That Works.* New York: Harper & Row, 1981.

Strunk, William, Jr., and E. B. White. *The Elements of Style,* 3rd ed. New York: Macmillan, 1979.

On Persuasion

Aristotle. *The Rhetoric and Poetics,* trans. W. Rhys Roberts. Modern Library Edition. New York: Random House, 1954.

Karlins, Marvin, and Herbert F. Abelson. *Persuasion: How Opinions and Attitudes Are Changed,* 2nd ed. New York: Springer, 1970.

Ogilvy, David. *Confessions of an Advertising Man.* New York: Atheneum, 1963.

———. *Ogilvy on Advertising.* New York: Crown Publishers, 1984.

Reeves, Rossner. *Reality in Advertising.* New York: Alfred A. Knopf, 1961.

Stone, Robert. *Successful Direct Mail Advertising and Selling.* Englewood Cliffs: Prentice-Hall, 1955.

On Consumer Behavior

Maslow, Abraham, ed. *Motivation and Personality,* 2nd ed. New York: Harper & Row, 1970.

Percy, Larry, and John R. Rossiter. *Advertising Strategy.* New York: Praeger, 1980.

Wasson, Chester R., and David H. McConaughy. *Buyer Behavior and Marketing Decisions.* New York: Appleton-Century-Crofts, 1968.

Notes

Chapter One

1. Camille Staciva, *Consumer Currents* (New York: Advertising to Women, Inc., 1984), pp. 3–9.
2. *Confessions of an Advertising Man* (New York: Atheneum, 1984), p. 110.
3. Thomas J. Peters and Robert H. Waterman, *In Search of Excellence: Lessons from America's Best-Run Companies* (New York: Harper & Row, 1982), p. 64. See also George A. Miller, "The Magical Number Seven, Plus or Minus Two: Some Limits on Our Capacity for Processing Information," *Psychological Review,* vol. 63 (1956), pp. 81–97.
4. *Ogilvy on Advertising* (New York: Crown Publishers, 1983), p. 10.

Chapter Two

1. *How to Win Friends and Influence People* (New York: Simon & Schuster, 1937), p. 55.
2. (New York: Alfred Knopf, 1961), p. 35.
3. Peters and Waterman, p. 64.
4. *The Rhetoric and Poetics,* trans. W. Rhys Roberts, (New York: Modern Library, Random House, 1954), p. 60.
5. Chester R. Wasson and David H. McConaughy, *Buyer Behavior and Marketing Decisions* (New York: Appleton-Century-Crofts, 1968), p. 161.

6. *How to Write, Speak, and Think More Effectively* (New York: Harper & Row, 1958), p. 39.
7. Walker Gibson, *Tough, Sweet and Stuffy* (Bloomington, Ind.: Indiana University Press, 1966).

Chapter Four

1. Dr. Siegfried Streufert, Pennsylvania State University College of Medicine, quoted in *The New York Times,* July 31, 1984, "Successful Executives Rely on Own Kind of Intelligence," by Daniel Goleman, p. C-1.
2. *Ogilvy on Advertising,* p. 16.
3. Marvin Karlins and Herbert F. Abelson, *Persuasion: How Opinions and Attitudes Are Changed,* 2nd ed. (New York: Springer, 1970), p. 99.
4. Karlins and Abelson, p. 90.
5. Larry Percy and John R. Rossiter, *Advertising Strategy* (New York: Praeger, 1980), p. 116.
6. Percy and Rossiter, p. 50.

Chapter Five

1. Robert Gunning, *The Technique of Clear Writing* (New York: McGraw-Hill, 1952).

Chapter Nine

1. James Atlas, "Beyond Demographics," *The Atlantic Monthly* (October 1984), pp. 49–55.
2. Atlas, pp. 52–53.

Chapter Ten

1. *Confessions of an Advertising Man,* pp. 105–106.

Index